# My

# Swan Lake

# Life

# My

AN

# Swan Lake

INTERACTIVE

# Life

HISTOIR

80,000 B.C.–MAY 31, 1965 A.D.

# Louise Blocker

L & L

PUBLISHERS

L&L Publishers
PO Box 4414
Culver City, CA 90231

ISBN: 978-1-7328347-0-5 pbk
ISBN: 978-1-7328347-1-2 ebk

*Editing and book design by Stacey Aaronson*

Printed in the United States of America

With the exception of historical figures and the author's relatives,
names of some individuals have been changed to protect
their privacy.

# DEDICATION

*Written for Lamin Josiah Williams,*
*this book is dedicated to his father, Jason Russell Williams,*
*and my nieces and nephews in each generation*

*⤳*

# IN MEMORIAM

*An inspiration to family and friends,*
*my mother,*
*Lula Johnson Blocker*

# CONTENTS

# Prelude

Despite the threat of an overcast April sky, my grandson Lamin and I followed our usual routine during my visit for spring break. After a light breakfast, we rushed to Toys 'R' Us to preview presents I might buy for his birthday upon returning to Atlanta in May. By the time we arrived and parked the car, so did a shower. Huddled under an umbrella, we ran inside and went directly to the LEGOs. After comparing three shelves of sets by age, design, and price, Lamin chose two designs. Then we browsed through several books, looked at Matchbox cars, and priced a couple of video games.

Pleased with our preview, we high-fived our way out of the store, ignoring the drizzle as we strolled across the parking lot, laughing and talking all the way to the car. Instead of immediately leaving for lunch, we sat awhile, boasting about the two LEGO sets he had selected. I like buying in pairs for myself, and I could do no less for my eight-year-old grandson. What a delightful time we were having!

Suddenly, there was a lull in the conversation. I glanced at Lamin, but he turned his head, so I waited for him to respond.

Several seconds passed before he softly said, "Grandmother Louise, I have a question."

Cheerfully, I answered, "Sure, sweetheart, what is it?"

"Uh, did you have any fun when you were a slave?" he asked.

I burst out laughing and questioned if my age was beginning to show. But the laughter vanished when I took a closer look and saw Lamin on the brink of tears, clenching his fingers and staring into space. His voice trembled when he tried to explain how old he thought I was. Unlike any I had ever seen, the sadness on his face seemed to have crushed his spirit. In an instant, the jovial atmosphere in the car became as gloomy as the sky.

Something in our outing must have triggered questions that had apparently haunted Lamin since African American History Month—questions he thought someone as old as I look now could answer. Clearly, he was stricken by the contrast between his life and his image of mine during slavery. However, he seemed less disturbed after I assured him I had not been a slave. Our conversation continued with Lamin smiling faintly as I described how enslaved Africans enjoyed playing games with their children, singing humorous songs, and telling stories.

EIGHT MONTHS LATER, after opening his last Christmas present, Lamin asked me what my childhood was like. Growing up as a tenant farmer's daughter in Mississippi, one of the poorest states in our country, I was one rung above slavery. Rather than bore the child with a long-winded speech about social classes and economic disparity, I gave him a short age-appropriate answer, emphasizing the fun of chasing rainbows, walking through puddles, and letting mud squish between my toes.

But considering Lamin's curiosity—and what he may not have learned during African American history month—I knew he deserved more than my knee-jerk response.

The following February, I decided to discuss both of his

questions further by writing a four- to five-page pamphlet. Well, after at least thirteen months of reviewing United States history and researching my ancestry, followed by a brief period of screening my juvenile escapades, I had enough material for two books—one history, the other a memoir. However, because many of the educational, social, and political conditions in our country during my childhood were a continuation of those that existed in my ancestors' time, it seemed fitting to combine their history with my coming-of-age memoir. I have attempted to do that in this book, aptly coined a *histoir*.

Before sitting down to write, I knew music would be included in the narrative, not only because of its role in my ancestors' lives, and in mine, but also to make the *histoir* interactive. I believed that engaging the reader with music would, at the least, create a virtual interaction. What's more, using a variety of songs would simulate an African tradition, and thereby honor my roots.

Today, like in the past, an oral historian and storyteller—known as a griot—takes his one-man show to villages in some areas of West Africa. In each village, he tells stories and recites local history, sometimes by singing and dancing. When the audience requests, he adds topical ballads to his repertoire of traditional songs, which he sings mostly from memory.

Entertained and informed by drums in Africa, but not allowed to use drums or their native language in America, enslaved Africans composed and sang songs to comfort, humor, and communicate with each other. They shared confidential information by singing songs with coded lyrics called Negro spirituals, our country's first original music.

Like the spirituals, blues and jazz are original genres of music created by African American composers. During my youth in Swan Lake, hot harmonicas in guitar-picking blues drove me to dance up a storm. Dirt flew all over our front yard when I boogied to Sonny Boy Williamson's "Good Morning Little School Girl." By the time I reached my teens in Memphis, Tennessee, I had begun to appreciate jazz, the result of having fallen in love with the famous singer-pianist Nat King Cole, and deciding he was the man I would marry.

While I am not a vocalist like Nat or a singing storyteller, in the tradition of the griot, I use titles of topical songs and instrumental pieces in the "Accompaniments" at the end of each chapter. In compliance with copyright laws, a link to the arrangements is not included. However, you can interact with this *histoir* by searching for the titles online, listening to the music, and "Dancing on the Ceiling."

Although my ancestry has been traced to 80,000 B.C., this narrative is not a comprehensive history. Rather, it is a summary of the most significant issues that affected the United States and my ancestors ages ago, and their lingering effects on my family and me through May 31, 1965 A.D.

To the best of my ability, I have kept the contents historically and scientifically correct, particularly the nomenclature. With an occasional exception, the terms Negro, colored, and African American are used in a historical context. In passages related to slavery, the words slave, enslaved African, and African are used interchangeably.

I am sure Lamin will forgive me when I digress and talk like the pedantic grandmother I am. I hope you will too.

# ♫ Accompaniments ♫

*Sung by the Soweto Gospel Choir, Bob Dylan's "Forever Young" speaks not only to his children for whom he wrote this song in 1972, but also to Lamin and children everywhere. If they stay forever young, they will remain inquisitive; preserve traditions to link past, present, and future; and become wise enough to recognize and support causes that are most beneficial to the world and its peoples.*

*Dylan's gift of the pen earned him the Nobel Prize for Literature in 2016. A songwriter and a singer, he became the first musician to receive this prestigious award.*

# A Pastoral Symphony

The first time I heard Beethoven's 6th Symphony, *Pastoral,* I was transported to scenes from my childhood: wide-open spaces, flowing creeks, patchy pastures, cows grazing, and a gravel road stretching from the beginning of one plantation to the end of another. Each of the symphony's movements was a video of my Swan Lake life.

From the early 1900s through 2013, Swan Lake was the postal address for the place where I was born, the Flautt Plantation in northwest Mississippi. Cotton, corn, and bean fields covered almost every acre. I saw those fields and so much more as I listened to the *Pastoral Symphony* in my music appreciation class at Dillard University.

In the first movement—Swan Lake in the spring—rays of sun streamed through clusters of the whitest clouds floating in the bluest sky. Green, leafy stalks filled each row of the cotton field on the right side of the gravel road; clusters of soybeans hugged every inch of soil in the bean field on the left. Dandelions, buttercups, and daffodils waltzed around the yard all the way to the edge of the dirt road in front of our house. Peppergrass and four-leaf clovers boogied in the pasture near the shotgun house of the plantation owner's cook.

A breeze blew through the weeping willow beside our

white brick house. The creek down the road glistened like a mirror. Up the road, fruit trees in the Flautts' orchard held buds that would burst into irresistible apricots, peaches, and plums in the summer, and juicy persimmons and apples in the fall.

In the next scene, our dog Blue lay under a shade tree in front of the run-down house where I was born. I stood in our yard, gazing at the sky and talking to a cloud that looked exactly like the only picture we had of my father. The cloud's movement was Daddy's response to me, and when its shape began to change, I knew he was waving bye-bye. I smiled and waved back. (Whenever I became frustrated, I looked at the clouds and talked, certain the one that resembled Daddy was somewhere among them.)

The second movement—Swan Lake on a day in May—was as refreshing as the breeze after a thunderstorm, which on a sunny day left at least one or two rainbows. Believing a pot of gold was at the end of each one, my sister Lorraine and I ran toward the closest rainbow, even into the woods. The longer we walked, the farther away the rainbow appeared. We never reached the gold because we could walk only so far before it was time to turn around to be home before dusk as Mother had told us.

The third movement—a scorching summer day—showed the iceman making his rounds, selling blocks of ice, and placing them in an insulated container called an icebox (refrigerators weren't yet common). Driving from one house to the next, he waved "howdy" to the men, women, and children chopping cotton, using a hoe to cut away weeds so the plants could thrive and grow into stalks spaced far enough apart for the cotton to be picked more easily. By mid-summer, the stalks were laden with green bulbs that would harden, turn brown, and become bolls filled with fluffy, white cotton, ready to pick in August.

How did we pick cotton?

Children used a thick sack about two feet wide and three or four feet long; adults used one twice that length. The bottom was reinforced with extra-heavy-duty burlap to reduce wear and tear from pulling the sack down the rows. A strap at the top of the sack was placed over the head to rest on the shoulder, leaving both hands free. Bending over, we would go down a row, quickly pull handfuls of cotton from the bolls on each side of the stalk, place the cotton into the sack, and periodically shake it down. At the end of the row, we would move to the next unpicked row, turn around, go up the row, and repeat this cycle until the sack was tightly packed all the way to the top. The sack became heavier the fuller it got, making it difficult to work quickly while trying to avoid the boll's knife-sharp tips.

The more cotton we picked, the more we earned. To the best of my memory, children received seventy-five cents for each sack of cotton picked and adults received a dollar per hundred pounds. On average, adults picked two to three hundred pounds a day. In two years, I picked an average of eighty-five pounds, up to ninety-two. By the end of October, all the cotton fit to be picked had been picked.

In the fourth movement—Swan Lake's transition from fall's foliage to winter's chills—green leaves burst into shades of yellow, red, orange, brown, and gold. Too soon, though, the trees would be coated in frost before becoming leafless as winter set in, which was slaughtering time. Calves and pigs squealed when my brothers led them to their execution, and my eldest sister Ethel Lee covered her ears and went to her house in tears—she could not stand to hear the animals cry. Mother, along with my sisters Sarah and Linda, mixed the ingredients to preserve the meat, a process called curing. For example, they cured the hog's hip to make ham, salted sections of the belly and back to make bacon and salt pork, and chopped and seasoned the head and jowls to make hog-head cheese, also called souse.

The fifth movement—a panorama of Swan Lake from the dawning to the yawning of day—showed light peeking through thin layers of clouds as the sky slowly dawned into a brilliant yellow-orange and blood-orange sunrise before turning crystal blue. A change in tempo brought images of clothes hanging on lines to dry; children running through puddles in their bare feet; and adults coming home from the field at the yawning of the day. Clusters of once-white clouds morphed into red-orange vapors that lingered until the sun became a scarlet ball, and in the blink of an eye, dove into the earth, leaving a red mist across a drowsy sky.

As the music faded, so did the day. Swan Lake's pitch-black nights were both frightening and fascinating: outside, we could see only our teeth when we talked, but we could see all the stars in the Milky Way, the craters and the man in the moon, the Big Dipper, the Little Dipper, and all their neighbors, whose names I used to know.

Like those long-gone names, so is the Swan Lake of my childhood. The five houses in my old neighborhood have been razed; the Flautts' house up the road from where I was born is still standing, but uninhabited; and only remnants of the orchard remain. The general store and post office no longer exist, nor does the airport that housed crop-dusting airplanes. Today, beans cover almost as many acres as cotton, which is now picked by machine. Employees instead of tenant farmers plant and harvest the crops.

Courtesy of the Flautts' generosity, as of this writing, ten African Americans—most of whom are retired—live in the northwestern section of the plantation. In 2013, they were as-signed mailboxes in Webb, Mississippi, the closest town, which is about seven miles north. To give you a picture of where that is, the closest city—Clarksdale, Mississippi—is eighteen miles north; Memphis, Tennessee, is 105 miles north.

## 🎵 Accompaniments 🎵

*Swan Lake will always be a Pastoral Symphony to me, but when Bob Flautt bought his property in the early 1900s, he may have thought of Tchaikovsky's ballet Swan Lake. How-ever, in the twelve and a half years I lived in Swan Lake, I never saw a ballet or a swan. And I didn't even know the eponymous lake existed until November 14, 1993. The lake is located in the northwestern section of the plantation; I lived on the northeastern side.*

# Dinosaur Days

## When I Was a Child

*Children knew their place*
*When I was a child.*
*They addressed adults as*
*Mr., Mrs., Miss, Aunt, or Uncle,*
*Answered, "Yes, ma'am,"*
*"Yes, sir," "No, ma'am," "No, sir."*
*Children were to be seen, not heard*
*When I was a child.*
*They spoke only when spoken to,*
*And to avoid a good*
*Talking-to that would leave them*
*Feeling mighty bad,*
*Children stayed in their place*
*When I was a child.*

Unlike when Lamin posed the question about fun during slavery, his face was all smiles when he asked, "Grandmother, what was it like when you were a kid?"

Well now, if one of my teachers in Swan Lake had heard him, she would have said, "Young man, a kid is a goat. Your grandmother was a child in my class, and I have no doubt she is rearing you to know better." Seeing him look confused, she would have explained, "Yes, rearing. Plants and animals are raised, children are reared."

She would have corrected him because in dinosaur days, our teachers taught in a manner to ensure we would not be seen as loud, uncouth, or unlearned—or rather, as the stereotypical image some people had of Negroes. Expecting us to be a "credit to our race" and a "good reflection on our family," they insisted we use the preferred definitions of words and speak in a well-modulated tone of voice. What's more, by addressing us as young men and young ladies, teachers gave us common courtesies that they knew we were not likely to receive from local whites when we became adults. Other grown-ups often addressed us as son, brother, sister, or daughter. Though no one ever explained this directly, they were building our self-esteem.

In addition to using homespun psychology to give us a sense of self-worth, Mother brought us up in the church, making sure we respected the house of worship not only by our behavior but also by our attire. Because it simply was not proper to wear what was called "everyday clothes" to church, she dressed us in our Sunday best: store-bought clothes or homemade dresses sewn from fine fabrics instead of muslin, and shoes polished until they shined like glass. Some of our home-sewn garments were as fine as designer apparel.

When we went to town, Sarah and Linda would gaze at dresses displayed in store windows. Back at home, they would take paper bags, make patterns, and place them on the material Mother had bought to make our Sunday clothes. Then they would cut the fabric, pin the parts of the dresses together, and sew them on our pedal sewing machine. Wearing our "designer" outfits, copies of the dresses displayed on mannequins, my sister Lorraine and I went to church feeling just a touch of pride.

My brothers J C and W C wore khakis and white shirts. (Yes, my brothers' names are letters, for which custom is the only explanation. Using letters for names was not unusual in dinosaur days.)

At church, we reviewed our Sunday school lesson before worship services began. From a blue booklet called a catechism, we learned about God's love for us and the rules He wanted us to follow. Besides loving and revering the only God, keeping the Sabbath holy, and honoring our parents, the most important rules were not to murder, steal, lie, or envy.

Except for flies, gnats, and worms, we did not kill. Other than the comic books and magazines Lorraine and I once took for revenge, fruit from the Flautts' orchard was the only thing we stole. (I'll tell you about the revenge in a few minutes, depending on how fast you read.) We did our best not to be jealous, and we did not lie. Why, we couldn't even say the word "lie" because it was considered profanity. But since we didn't use "big words" like "profanity," a lie was called a "story," "curse word," or "bad word."

Worship began with an opening prayer and at least two slow and reflective songs, such as "Shine on Me" or "I Love the Lord." A deacon sang part of a verse, which the congregation repeated; then he sang the second part, and the congregation repeated it. This cycle continued until each verse had been sung. The deacon led the congregation because many people could not read at the time the songs were written. Later on, some rural churches either did not have hymnals or did not have enough.

While the congregation sang the opening hymn, Mother and the other ushers took their positions: two opened the doors to the sanctuary; the others directed people to their seats. Smiling faintly as she greeted worshippers, Mother looked angelic in her crisp, white uniform, white usher's cap, white socks, white shoes, and white gloves. With no makeup, her smooth caramel complexion was radiant.

A solo by a choir member with a beautiful voice was my favorite part of the service. Listening to the choir was enough church for me, but we could not leave before the pastor gave the benediction, after which everyone stood and sang "God Be with You." How I loved that reassuring song, but I could hardly wait to get home for our weekly feast, Sunday dinner.

Often, ministers went to a member's home for Sunday dinner. W C told me this story about one of Mother's pastors who prefaced his visits by announcing, "Now, when I come for dinner, I want chicken. I don't eat no rabbit."

Mother refrained from work on Sunday, the Sabbath for most Christians. On Saturday, she did chores such as pressing her usher's uniform and preparing most of Sunday's dinner. The Saturday before the pastor came to our house, W C and J C went hunting, caught some rabbits, and dressed them. By sundown on Saturday, Mother had washed the rabbit in a solution of vinegar and water, sprinkled a little salt and pepper on each piece, rolled the pieces in seasoned flour, and fried them. Then she made her signature brown gravy and simmered the fried rabbit in it until each piece was melt-in-your-mouth tender.

On Sunday, she served the rabbit with the usual fixings: a red leaf lettuce, cucumber, and tomato salad; sautéed squash; butter beans; homemade rolls; and peach cobbler for dessert.

The pastor ate heartily. On his way to the door, he thanked Mother, saying, "Sister Blocker, that was some really good chicken. Best chicken I had in a long time!"

Smiling, Mother replied, "Pastor, that wasn't chicken. That was rabbit."

His eyes bulging with horror, the minister gave Mother a

half-baked smile and a limp handshake as he donned his hat and stepped through the doorway. Seems he couldn't make it off the porch fast enough.

Whether she tricked the preacher or not, I don't know, but I do know Mother wasn't pretentious. Glad to share whatever she had, Mother would have considered it wasteful to cook a chicken for the minister and rabbit for everyone in the family, except for me (I would be happy with only vegetables, other than okra or eggplant). Mother thought what she prepared for her family was good enough for anyone who chose to join us.

On what was left of Sunday afternoon, having spent all morning through mid-afternoon in church, the adults played checkers and had grown-up conversations in the front room—called the living room today—while we children played in a back room or outdoors.

The boys played with their yo-yos, slingshots, wooden guns, or BB guns; the girls enjoyed shoo-fly, Little Sally Walker, or ring around the roses. I have forgotten how we played shoo-fly, but not Little Sally Walker. Holding hands, the girls formed a circle and sang as they walked around one girl who sat on the ground in the middle of the circle, the imaginary saucer.

*Little Sally Walker, sitting in a saucer,*
*Weeping and crying for a cool drink of water.*
*Rise, Sally, rise.*
*Wipe your weeping eyes.*
*Put your hands on your hips*
*and let your backbone slip.*
*Now you shake it to the east.*
*Aw, shake it to the west.*
*Aw, shake it to the one that you love the best.*

The one sitting in the saucer followed the directions in the song, and when she shook it to the one she loved the best, she pointed to a girl and said, "My mama told me to pick you." That girl then took her turn in the saucer and the game continued until every girl had a turn, each one trying to outdo the other. We laughed and shook our little behinds with complete abandon. This game was passed down from slavery, with the third line changed from "weeping and crying for someone to love her" to "weeping and crying for a cool drink of water."

"The dozens" was another not-so-innocent game, but we sneaked and played it because our parents had warned us not to let them catch us "playing the dozens." In the game, two players tease each other by exchanging jokes about their looks, intelligence, or relatives. The object of the game is to make the most creative or humiliating taunt. Players are egged on by onlookers' applause and laughter. The teasing becomes progressively heated, and so do the players. Ultimately one of them is stumped and responds with two game-ending words, as in this example:

*First player:* "Your legs are so long you can walk a mile with only two steps."

*Second player:* "Yours are so short you can't keep up with a snail."

*First player:* "I may be slow, but you can't spell book, let alone read one."

*Second player:* "And you can't add two plus three."

*First player:* "At least the mirror winks at me. Show your face, and it cracks up."

*Second player:* "Your mama."

The onlookers gasp! The players' fists start flying, one of them starts crying, and two or three onlookers break up the fight. Had the second player exercised self-control and made his last response a smile instead of an insult, he would have lost the game but avoided a fight. However, the smile would have made him the object of ridicule.

So, what is the origin of this wicked game?

The practice of selling slaves who were handicapped—or past their prime—in groups of twelve is thought to be the origin of "the dozens," a custom enslaved Africans considered disrespectful and humiliating. "Dozen," a Scottish word that means "to stun," may be the origin of the game's name: an exceptionally quick, witty, and skillfully phrased taunt stuns a player, leaving him to resort to the game-ending words, "your mama." Makes me wonder how in the world a Scottish word became associated with a game typically linked to African American culture. Must be the six degrees of separation theory.

I do not remember "playing the dozens," but like everyone in my family, I listened to programs on the radio, stories that were like situation comedies we see on TV today. In Swan Lake, we did not have a TV or even know it existed. Every Saturday after supper, I listened to programs, quickly did the dishes, and waited for Mother to recite Negro folklore or to tell us stories about Brer Bear and Brer Rabbit.

Hoping to have rabbit for dinner, Brer Bear sets traps to catch Brer Rabbit, but he never does because Brer Rabbit outsmarts him with a trick. Found in Joel Chandler Harris's book, *Uncle Remus*, the stories are fables Harris based on African tales he overheard in enslaved Africans' conversations. Brer Bear represents the slaveholder. A dual character, Brer Rabbit symbolizes the master who cannot be trusted or the slave who outwits his master with feigned dimwittedness.

At bedtime, we knelt, said our prayers, and pleaded for Linda, the best storyteller in our family, to tell us another story. She had a way of taking us from uproarious laughter to paralyzing fear. Her specialty was stories about ghosts, called "haints" in Swan Lake and other areas in the South too. Oh, how we would laugh when she made funny faces and did the haint's dance!

About halfway through the story, Linda would dangle her arms and twist her neck while rolling her eyes, making scary sounds and grimacing like a haint. We would put our heads under the covers, stick our fingers in our ears, and close our eyes. Rarely did we make it to the end of the story, but we repeated the ritual the following Sunday just the same.

During the week, we were back in church as students. Before 1950, there were no public schools in the area for Negroes. Any colored person with a grade-school education could teach in the church schools, particularly those located in rural areas. (The schools did not offer religious instruction: churches were merely used because no other buildings were as suitable or available to Negroes for schools.) Having completed eight years of schooling, my sister Sarah taught first through eighth grade at our church school. I was one of her students in the first and second grades.

In 1949, ground was broken to build a public grade school on the lot adjacent to our church. To teach in public schools, teachers were required to have a grammar or high school diploma and two years of education at a normal school, one that trained teachers. The term "normal school" was chosen because the schools set the norm for classroom instruction, particularly knowledge of subject matter, methods of teaching, and practice teaching. Sadly, Sarah could not continue as a teacher because she did not have the money to attend a normal school.

When Swan Lake's Negro public school opened in September, 1950, I no longer had to share one room with students of all ages. Instead, I had my own third-grade classroom and a beautiful teacher named Mrs. Rachael Scurlock. Miss Rachael, as we called her, was kind and patient. She never raised her voice, and she treated us like we were her own children.

Our day at school began with devotion: a passage from the Bible, usually the Lord's Prayer or the Twenty-Third Psalm; the Pledge of Allegiance, recited with our right hands placed over our hearts; and a patriotic song, such as "God Bless America." These spiritual and citizenship exercises were accompanied by adages written on the blackboard every Monday morning, each meant to give the brain cells a workout. Students could volunteer or wait to be called on to explain proverbs such as "hitch your wagon to star," "a rolling stone gathers no moss," "the early bird gets the worm," "don't put all your eggs in one basket," or "don't be a fair-weather friend."

After devotion, we read and studied arithmetic, geography, health, and history. Then we practiced cursive writing. Years ago, Miss Rachael told me my writing was so tiny she could barely read it—that was because I tried to prevent my classmates from seeing me write.

Our church school did not have desks, so we wrote with a pad on our laps. Like most schools at the time, our new school had only right-handers' desks. Being left-handed—until I learned to angle the paper with the lower right corner pointing toward my navel—I had to position my hand and arm in a way that my classmates found amusing. If you saw a news clip of President Obama signing a document, you have seen the position of which I speak. Writing in that position resulted in smaller penmanship and my classmates' ridicule. Uncomfortable in the right-hander desk and fed up with the teasing, I stopped writing in class. Instead, I practiced cursive writing at home and made pretending to write at school part of my fantasy world.

I could hardly wait until May Day, the date of our end-of-school program. What a fun-filled day of games, songs, and recitations! Oh, how I loved the dramatic readings of James Weldon Johnson's "The Creation" and Paul Lawrence Dunbar's "When Malindy Sings!"

The fun continued at our annual picnic for our relatives who had migrated to the North. Cousins Johnny B. Powell and May Laura came from Detroit. Cousins in nearby towns also came to fellowship and enjoy the food that Mother, Ethel, Sarah, and Linda had prepared. B (my oldest brother, known by his middle name, the letter B) provided the entertainment, and he never looked more handsome than when playing his guitar. All the adults danced, except for Mother. Children competed in dance contests, which I never won. Left-handed and left-footed, I turned right when everyone else turned left, and I stepped with my left foot when they stepped with their right. What a sight!

Picnics were the highlights of summer, but Christmas was the best time of the entire year, especially when it snowed. While it was never icy cold in Swan Lake, at the first sign of snow, we would place a bucket outside to catch snow for Mother and Sarah to make snow cream. Sometimes they would also scoop the top layer of snow from the ground, make sure it was clean, place it in a bowl, and stir in a little milk, vanilla flavor, and whatever else they thought would make it taste good. And it always did, but not quite as good as the ice cream they made in the summer.

We did not have a Christmas tree, but we definitely believed in Santa Claus. Every year, he brought us a crocus-sack stocking stuffed with some hard candy—usually peppermint—nuts, a Red Delicious apple, and a large navel orange. In the good years, Santa almost always bought rag dolls for Lorraine and me and toy guns for J C and W C. Mother gave us new clothes, but only those we needed. She emphasized the importance of being grateful for what we had and not thinking about what we lacked. It was hard to think that way most of the time, but not at Christmas. I tell you, even to this day, the spirit of Christmas turns my blues into rock and roll!

## ♫ Accompaniments ♫

*Listening to Sam Cooke and the Soul Stirrers' "Wonderful" always takes me back to church in Swan Lake, and Selah's "God Be with You" brings a smile of gratitude as I remember the wonderful Sunday dinner that waited for us at home.*

*The rapper of my day, Louis Jordan, turned nursery rhymes of my time into "School Days," and he made poultry talk in "Ain't Nobody Here but Us Chickens." A great saxophonist too, he had food rapping in "Beans and Corn Bread," and all the farm animals jiving in "Barnyard Boogie."*

*Man, oh man, no one blew the clarinet and trombone like Tommy Dorsey! How we danced to his "Boogie Woogie!" When his horns came through the radio or from the record on our Victrola, I jumped up to cut a rug with Lorraine and my nieces Annette, Bettie, and Jean, who had all mastered the boogie-woogie—a fast-paced dance with lots of twists and turns. But my version gave the dance a bad name.*

# Who We Are

On dinosaur days, I was taught three races of people populated the earth. Since then, I have learned that "race" is merely a concept, which at best attempts to answer the question: Why the difference in appearance and customs among folks around the world?

At worst, the notion of race, as the word implies, pits human beings against each other, with some claiming to be superior. According to literature I read about the scientists credited with racial classifications, *race* was not the term they used in classifying human beings: one used *group*, the other, *variety*.

Swedish botanist Carl Linnaeus (1707–1778) first classified all human beings as *Homo sapiens*, which means wise man in Latin—the language used in international communications, academia, and science during his time. He then identified *Homo sapiens* as four geographical *groups*.[1] Linnaeus did not rank the groups, but he gave Europeans a competitive edge by adding his perception of each group's physical, social, and emotional traits.[2]

- *Native Americans* – reddish, erect, obstinate
- *Europeans* – white, sanguine, gentle
- *Asians* – sallow, melancholy, avaricious
- *Africans* – black, relaxed, crafty, negligent

Similarly, German anatomist Johann Blumenbach (1752–1840) described five *varieties* of human beings, attributing the difference in their physical features to culture and climate and finding no difference in intellectual abilities.[3] Nevertheless, he listed his varieties in hierarchical order beginning with the one he thought most physically attractive.

- *Caucasians* – fair-skinned people in Europe and in adjacent parts of Asia and Africa. Note: Europe is known as a continent because the Caucasus Mountain Range is considered a geographical barrier between it and Asia, the location of the three ranges that comprise the Caucasus. Blumenbach thought the skull of a white female found in the mountain range the most beautiful in his collection of 60 skulls.[4]

- *Mongolians* – Asians, including the Japanese and Chinese

- *Ethiopians* – dark-skinned Africans

- *Americans* – most native people in the New World (Western Hemisphere)

- *Malays* – Polynesians, Melanesians, and aborigines of Australia

Geography was the initial method by which Linnaeus and Blumenbach differentiated human beings. However, both strayed from the protocol for legitimate scientific inquiry by adding immeasurable and subjective features such as character traits, skin color, and physical attractiveness. In scientific studies, any change in the method, materials, or subjects renders the results invalid. Such is the case with the Caucasoid (white), Mongoloid (red/yellow), and Negroid (black) races I learned about in elementary school. Two are named for geographical areas; one for skin color. Now, you may be wondering, "Why these three *races* instead of Blumenbach's five *varieties* or Linnaeus's four *groups?*"

To the best of my understanding, these "races" may be attributed to the observations of anthropologists Franz Boas (1858–1942) and Alfred L. Kroeber (1876–1960).[5] Viewing the world as a sphere with the Indian Ocean on one side and the Pacific Ocean on the other, Boas labeled people on the lands touching the Indian Ocean Negroid because they had dark complexions, strongly developed jaws, relatively long arms, and kinky or fuzzy hair. He identified as Mongoloid people in lands reaching the Pacific Ocean because they were light-skinned with straight hair, relatively short arms, and slight jaws. Kroeber proposed classifying the lighter-skinned people in Europe as a distinct race, Caucasoid.

So, how did the word race come to be used in describing people? Well, let's take a look . . .

According to the Online Etymology Dictionary, race was not used in the context of grouping people until the sixteenth century. From 1200 through the 1400s, the definition of race referred to motion: running, speed, and competition, as in a race of speed. In the 1500s, the Middle French word race meant "people of a common descent," i.e., "breed, lineage, family." The word r*ace* went through quite a metamorphosis in English:

- Early 1300s – act of running
- 1500 – common occupation, people, or group
- 1510 – contest of speed
- 1520 – wines with characteristic flavor
- 1540 – generation

- 1560 – tribe, nation, people regarded from common stock

- 1774 – one of the great divisions of mankind based on physical peculiarities

As far as I can determine, people identified themselves by culture, family, nation, or tribe before scientists attempted to answer the question of diversity among the earth's peoples. Today, *ethnicity* appears to be replacing *race*, a by-product of man's competitive nature, which, among more issues than this discussion can address, created the question of who we are for the United States's third largest ethnic group.

Prior to the early 1960s, melanin-rich Americans of African descent were called *Negro* or *colored*. *Negro* was used exclusively until *colored* was introduced in the 1800s, probably to recognize mulattoes, individuals whose parents were of different "races," one black, the other white. Today, such offspring are called biracial.

By 1900, *Negro* and *colored* were used interchangeably, with *colored* gaining a slight advantage after the founding of the National Association for the Advancement of Colored People (NAACP) in 1909. This may have been the first and only case of capitalizing colored. Probably in response to Negro activists, particularly W.E.B Du Bois, the *New York Times* began capitalizing "negro" when referring to *race* in 1939. More about Du Bois later.

After the slogan "Black is beautiful" became popular in the 1960s, *black* and the label *Afro-American* competed for acceptance in the 1970s. Although calling a Negro "black" had always been considered rude, *black* won. In 1988, *African American* made its debut. Currently, both *black* and *African American*

are used, but the latter appears to be preferred by the powers-
that-be, whose identity is a mystery to me. Nevertheless, I
think their rationale for changing who we are is threefold: an
aversion to the word negro, an assertion of the right to self-
classify, and a proclamation of the heritage slavery claimed.

The negative connotations in the definition of the color
black certainly are not appealing. The concept *race* was almost
three centuries in the future when the Portuguese used negro,
their word for black, to describe the Africans' color. The label
"Negro" represents a time when slaveholders may have used
"niger," the Latin word for black, or addressed a slave who appeared to be stingy or mean as "niggardly." Some white people
may have mispronounced negro as "negra" or "nigger." In the
"Negro community," nigger was defined as any disrespectful,
uneducated member of a lower social class, particularly a person
seen as rude, boisterous, or vulgar, sometimes called a shiftless
or trifling good-for-nothing. The mispronunciation is an ethnic slur; the covert definition is slang.

During the Civil Rights Movement (1955–1964), colored
people sought not only equal opportunity in the United States,
but also a means to connect with the motherland and thereby
reclaim their heritage. Records of kidnapped Africans' names
and where they were captured or born in Africa are virtually
nonexistent. Considered as property, Africans were not issued
birth certificates in the United States. Except for United States
federal censuses from 1860 forward, documents with enslaved
Africans' names, dates, and places of birth in our country are
rare. Consequently, most melanin-rich Americans of African
descent cannot trace their ancestry to a nation or a tribe in
Africa. Thus, many embrace the entire continent and accept
the label African American to honor their African ancestry and
to acknowledge their American citizenship.

Perhaps the next change will be *American African,* to distinguish citizens who are descendants of Africans enslaved in our country from naturalized melanin-rich citizens who emigrated from African countries. Technically, and to eliminate the question of who they are, those new citizens' country of birth should precede American. As for me, although "Black" is shown on my birth certificate, I don't wear the color well, so I will continue to write *human* in the space allotted for *race/ethnicity.*

## ♫ Accompaniments ♫

*Based on the success of organ transplants across racial lines, it seems more scientists in the medical community see humans as "Different Colours/One People." Lucky Dube's vocals and rhythm on this song complement not only this chapter but also Lamin's African and Jamaican roots.*

*Speaking on research, cell biologist and Nobel Prize winner Yoshinori Oshumi (1945) said, "There is no finish line for science. When I find the answer to one question, another question comes up." Such was the case for me with this chapter. Finding no biblical or scientific basis for "race," I was left with the question: Was it a coincidence to define race as "people of a common descent" at about the same time Africans were classified as cargo in the Transatlantic slave trade?*

*While Stevie Wonder may see the answer "Blowin' in the Wind," like the singer Johnny Nash, I simply accept that "There Are More Questions Than Answers."*

# The Evolution of American Slavery

or the purpose of this discussion, it is appropriate to note that some form of slavery has existed since the beginning of time.

The Hebrews' bondage in Egypt, one of the earliest accounts, is documented in the Bible (Exodus 1:8–14) with the story of Pharaoh, an Egyptian king, who felt threatened by the Hebrews' growing population. As a result, he placed ruthless managers over them, gave them the worst jobs, and ordered their midwives to kill all newborn Jewish males. But two clever women, Shiphrah and Puah, defied his order. They told Pharaoh that by the time they arrived, the babies were already born because, unlike Egyptian women, Jewish women had their babies quickly.

In areas worldwide, including Arabia, China, Great Britain, Greece, Japan, and Rome, people with power and privilege kept those of a lower socioeconomic status or different ethnicity in some form of binding servitude, such as serfs to work the land, servants to clean castles, and nursemaids to take care of children. In some parts of Africa, victors of tribal wars took the losers as captives, kept several as servants, and sold others to Arabia. (Selling disgruntled captives who could have escaped and returned to their own villages was less trouble than keeping them.) But despite their status, slaves in Africa could marry and keep their children, who, in contrast to offspring in America, were not considered slaves.

During the Middle Ages (c.500 to 1400–1500), Germanic men in northern Europe captured and sold so many individuals from central, eastern, and southern Europe that the people living in those areas became known as Slavs, giving birth to the word *slave*.[1] Because they were not affiliated with organized religion, the Slavs were considered pagans whom Christians could enslave without violating the doctrine forbidding the enslavement of fellow Christians.

With non-Muslim men from Arabia, however, it seems creeds against human bondage did not apply. In the sixth century, Arabia invaded Nubia and enslaved its people. (An ancient kingdom, Nubia was located in the Nile Valley of Southern Egypt and Northern Sudan.) Muslim Arabs entered the African slave trade in the seventh century and monopolized the market until Portugal became a competitor in 1444, a by-product of the search for an alternate route to the Far East.[2]

To meet Europeans' growing demand for China's silk, fine porcelain, and precious gems, as well as India's healing herbs and savory spices, merchants sought a route to bring those products to market as quickly and safely as possible. If not faster, a route by sea would eliminate the hazards of traveling through areas in central Europe and the Middle East where salesmen were targets for robbery, and two or more countries were either engaged in warfare or terrorizing each other.

Portugal's Prince Henry the Navigator (1394–1460), a navigator of commerce not of the waterways, sponsored multiple expeditions, hoping to reach the Far East by sea. Portuguese sailors, the best in the world at that time, traveled south on the Atlantic Ocean along the west coast of Africa and around the

Cape of Good Hope to reach not only India and the Far East, but also to gain access to Africa's natural resources, particularly gold.[3]

Portuguese seamen were the first Europeans to arrive in Benin, a prosperous kingdom in southwestern Nigeria. Impressed by the well-designed city and the elegant palace with guards posted at the entrance, the Portuguese made a deal with the king: an exchange of alcoholic beverages, guns, and ammunition for ivory, gold, peppers, and people. Thus began the Euro-African slave trade, better known as the Transatlantic slave trade—a boon for the banking, insurance, and ship-building industries in Spain, France, Great Britain, and the Netherlands, the major competitors for kidnapped Africans.

Spain's entry into the Transatlantic slave trade can be attributed to the Italian sailor Christopher Columbus (1451–1506)—Cristoforo Columbo in Italian—who lost his way trying to reach the Far East by sailing west. He thought going west across the Atlantic would be a safer and shorter route than sailing south like the Portuguese had done. But although he was a mapmaker himself, Columbus was mistaken. To cover up his blunder and persuade his copilots not to abort the voyage, Columbus altered the ship's log to show less than the actual number of miles traveled.[4] In fact, had a ribbon of Caribbean Islands not been seen within forty-eight hours as he promised, his copilots would have returned to Europe. When his ship landed at the island he named El Salvador, Columbus claimed it and the adjacent islands for Spain, calling them the West Indies because he thought they were off the west coast of India. According to some historians, Columbus died believing he had reached the Far East, but I am not convinced. Just like he misrepresented the number of miles traveled to save face, Columbus more than likely created this story to get his ten percent share of the "riches" he found and to appease his sponsors, Spain's Queen Isabella (1474–1504) and King Ferdinand (1452–1516).[5]

Having rejected Columbus's proposed voyage three times, the king and queen agreed to finance it only after Isabella's priest, Juan Perez (?–1513) interceded on his behalf. Not only did Columbus ensure his take by kidnapping and transporting indigenous people back to Spain and boasting about the riches found on the Caribbean Islands, he also changed the focus from seeking a shorter route to the Far East to claiming land, precious jewels, and gold nuggets in the New World, hereafter called the Americas.

Hoping to improve their lives, opportunists, former landowners, farmers, servants, convicts, religious reformers, the naïve, and the noble immigrated to the Americas. After settling in their newly built log cabins, the immigrants—better known as colonists—had to import European products until they could make their own furnishings and produce enough goods for both consumption and sales. To do that, they needed reliable workers.

Most of their helpers were European indentured servants, who, after completing their term of indenture—usually five to seven years—set out to stake claims and pan for gold themselves. Thus, not only did the demand for indentured servants exceed the supply, it also would have been futile to bring more laborers from Europe.

What to do?

Initially, the colonists, the majority of whom were British immigrants, replaced indentured servants with Irish immigrants and Native Americans, attempting to enslave both. When that failed, the colonists turned to another source from which to obtain labor: European slave traders who, like the

Portuguese had done in Benin, made a deal with a few corrupt African chiefs and a small number of greedy slave dealers. Consequently, the immigrants secured not only a free labor force but one thought to be permanent as well. For unlike Native Americans, whose familiarity with the lay of the land facilitated their successful escapes, Africans were trapped by skin color and geography. They could not blend in with Native Americans or sympathetic colonists, and they could not dash across the Atlantic Ocean to their homelands.

The Africans' physical condition also offered a degree of reliability. To ensure the healthiest and most physically fit individuals were purchased, European slave traders examined the Africans from the tops of their heads to the bottoms of their feet before marching them, in shackles and muzzles, from their captors to ports on the West Coast of Africa. The ship's doctor reexamined the Africans before allowing them to board, leaving those deemed unseaworthy to the mercy of African slave dealers.

Having overcome their trek to the coast and the deplorable conditions on slave ships, Africans often survived illnesses that some whites and Native Americans did not—which left the colonists perplexed. Instead of seeing the Africans' survival as an attribute, however, it seems most of the colonists perceived it and the Africans' physical features to mean they were inferior. Perhaps whites who considered themselves superior were merely projecting their own feelings of inferiority to justify dehumanizing Africans, and thereby absolve themselves of the immoral practice of slavery.

Comparing Africans to whites based on resistance to disease was unfair to say the least. Only the healthiest Africans were brought to the Americas. Although hearty, some of the Europeans certainly came with issues. More than likely, poor

farmers were malnourished before leaving Europe, and afflu-
ent immigrants probably bore emotional scars from the religious persecution they left Europe to escape. Criminals and
those forcibly shipped to the colonies were probably not in
great health, either. As for Native Americans, many of them
succumbed to European diseases such as syphilis and smallpox
to which they had never been exposed.

Africans who escaped smallpox probably had been inoculated against the dreaded disease in Africa. The description of a
procedure Africans used to cure smallpox is similar to the
smallpox vaccinations given throughout the world from the
mid-1800s until 1980, when the World Health Organization
declared smallpox eradicated. Puritan minister Cotton Mather
(1663–1728) learned about this procedure from one of his
African-born slaves whose name was replaced with a biblical
one, Onesimus.

Like many people did at the time, Mather kept a diary, and
he recorded what Onesimus told him about an old African cure
for smallpox[6]: pricking the pustules that formed from the rash
released pus, a drop of which when placed in a small cut or
scratch on a healthy person's skin, exposed him to the smallpox
virus and made him immune to the disease. The "inoculation"
also left a scar. Onesimus showed Mather the one that formed
on his arm after the procedure was performed on him when he
was a child.

During the 1721 smallpox epidemic in Boston, Mather
discussed Onesimus's smallpox "inoculation" with a doctor
friend. The doctor inoculated his own son and two slaves and
they remained healthy, so he proceeded to vaccinate more
people. Only 2 percent of those vaccinated died, but 15 percent
of those not inoculated succumbed to the disease.

Legally prohibited from applying for a patent, Onesimus

has never been formally recognized for his role in eradicating smallpox. Instead, British scientist Edward Jenner is acknowledged as having discovered the smallpox vaccination in 1796, over thirty years after Onesimus introduced the procedure.

It is not known if Jenner knew about the African cure, but it is clear the Europeans' perception of their African captives changed slavery from a condition based on socioeconomic status to one based on race. And to maintain their privileged status, white immigrants used slave labor to build an economy that transformed the pristine land of independent nations into a leading world power.

## ♫ Accompaniments ♫

*Thought to be the second man-made musical instrument, the wooden flute is reserved for males only in the Lakota nation. However, composer Paul La Roche's daughter Nicole has mastered a technique on the metal classical flute that produces a nearly indistinguishable sound on "Star People" from Robert Mirabal's wooden flute on "Lullaby." This young lady really rocks on "One World, One Nation" and "Dance of Life."*

*Adopted by a white couple who recognized his talent and supported his musical pursuits, La Roche learned he was Lakota after they died—within the same year. After a multi-year period of mourning both the loss of his adoptive parents and his biological heritage, La Roche moved his family to the Lower Brulè Reservation in South Dakota, where many of his Lakota relatives live. His compositions—a blend of sixties' rock* 'n roll, pop, jazz, and traditional Native American music—may best be described as New Age soul. He tours with his band Brulè and an entourage of Lakota dancers. A La Roche concert is one not to miss, not only for the dancing and music but also for his storytelling!

# Whence and How They Came

Hoping to identify my ancestors, where they lived in Africa, and when they were brought to America, I had my DNA (deoxyribonucleic acid) analyzed. Interestingly, although this genetic material carried in each of our chromosomes becomes mixed over time, some of it remains the same in all generations of people who have a common ancestor. To determine this connection, a technician uses a microscope to look at cells, such as those in samples of bodily fluids, hair follicles, skin, etc. Cells in samples from different individuals with identical segments of DNA on one or both copies of their twenty-three pairs of chromosomes indicate the individuals are descendants of a common ancestor.

The first analysis of my DNA identified segments on my chromosomes matching those of a woman who lived in Northeast Africa around 80,000 B.C. She hailed from the area known to have traded ebony, ivory, leather, and metal for salt, frankincense, and myrrh from Arabia. Perhaps her offspring lived in Kush, known as Ethiopia today.[1] Apparently, some of her descendants migrated throughout Africa and even into Europe.

Subsequent analyses found some of my genetic material identical to that of individuals in Ghana, Cameroon, Mali, Nigeria, South-Central Africa, Great Britain, Spain, and Portugal. Although shocked by the discovery of my European ancestry, I was pleased to have names for the places whence my African ancestors came. Those from South-Central Africa and Nigeria lived among farmers and artisans who were the first to smelt iron, use the plow, develop irrigation systems, and rotate crops.[2] Considering the wooden toys Daddy made, I could relate to Nigerian artists who turned pieces of wood, ivory, and stone into fine sculptures.

Having roots in Ghana and Mali, the most prosperous kingdoms in Africa during the Middle Ages, certainly made me proud. Both countries enjoyed a healthy economy from taxes levied on products exchanged between sub-Saharan African merchants and Arabian businessmen. But before getting too puffed up, I discovered that by the sixteenth century, those taxes were not only on commodities such as ebony, gold, ivory, kola nuts, leather, and metal, but also on children, men, and women whom African slave dealers sold to European slave traders—captains of ships—for cloth, muskets, whiskey, utensils, and ammunition.[3]

I don't know which of my ancestors slave traders purchased to sell to their countrymen who had claimed land in the Americas; however, because my great-grandparents' ages indicate they were slaves, it is likely their parents and grandparents were among the diverse group of Africans who were muzzled, chained, and shuffled to Africa's west coast. (I will tell you more about my great-grandparents' route to Swan Lake later.) At the coast, the Africans were displayed, examined, and crammed into a structure built to house them while sales were transacted. Once sold, the captives were branded and held on board until the captain had enough passengers to fill his slaver, a ship built specifically for transporting slaves.

After coming aboard, the Africans descended a stairwell to

the hold, a compartment between the lowest deck and the bottom of the ship. Keeping the Africans in the hold protected the crew, not only while the ship was on the African coast, but also on the Middle Passage, the area of the Atlantic Ocean from the northwest coast of Africa to ports in the Americas.

The journey across the Atlantic could take weeks or months, depending on weather, the experience of the ship's crew, and the Doldrums—an area in the Mid-Atlantic with periods of little or no wind that caused ships to sail at a snail's pace. Charged with maintaining the ship and overseeing hundreds of enslaved Africans, the crew had to guard against mutiny—only the gate to the hold protected them from their passengers.

The African men were shackled in pairs, with one man's right leg attached to another's left. On some slavers, the men were chained by the ankle, wrist, and neck. In the hold, the men were stacked on shelves without enough space to sit up straight.[4] They were able to sit erect or stand only when the crew brought them on deck and forced them to dance for exercise. The more physically fit the Africans appeared to be upon their arrival in the Americas, the higher their selling price.

Children and females were separated from the African men, making access to unshackled women easier for the captain and crew, as evidenced by some women giving birth to fair-skinned babies within a few months of their arrival in America. Obviously, the infants were fathered by Europeans who had sailed back to their homes by the time their offspring were born.

While the thought of thousands of children left to be reared by single mothers may be disturbing, it is important to remember that most whites who advocated slavery considered Africans inferior, except in clandestine affairs. Among those

who saw Africans as equals, the majority did not publicly sanc-
tion interracial relationships, let alone mixed marriages, which
were illegal in most areas of our country. Those "fatherless"
children were financial gains for whoever bought their mothers: two slaves for the price of one. It is unthinkable that any
of my ancestors may have been so violated or witnessed such
abuse.

On the other hand, their survival amidst some of the most
inhumane conditions—lack of privacy, pitiful housekeeping,
barely palatable food, inadequate medical care, fetid water—is
truly remarkable. Many others died from despair, dehydration,
disease, infections, and starvation; some perished from suffo-
cating in their cramped quarters or from choking while being
force-fed.5 Miserable but motivated, the Africans rebelled, indi-
vidually and collectively, attempting suicide or murder, refusing to take orders, attacking crew members, and trying to take
control of the ship. Until netting was put around the decks to
prevent group suicides, when an attempt on mutiny failed, the
individuals who planned the revolt jumped overboard together.

Despite failed attempts, revolts continued. Data at slave
voyages.org for the period 1730 through 1808 show over 400
under the category "African resistance." Various phrases, including "slave insurrections," "vessel attacked from the shore,"
and "cut off by Africans from the shore" are used to describe
the Africans' attempt to escape or to abort the voyage. Most of
their efforts failed, but let's look at a few that succeeded.

After overseeing the boarding of ninety-six African
men who had been purchased in Sierra Leone, Captain
George Scott began his voyage back to Rhode Island
on June 1, 1730. Five days later, he found himself facing two Africans who, having cast off their shackles,

defied his waving pistol, attacked him and three crew members, and held them captive until their fellowmen had sailed the *Little George* back to the Sierra Leone River. The Africans swam to shore, leaving the captain and crew with the abandoned ship. His life spared, Scott later recorded an account of his misadventure.

Captain Thomas Fear faced a similar fate in 1763. Data at slavevoyages.org indicate that the 169 Africans he was attempting to transport to the Americas disembarked on native land after the *Hope* was "attacked at the shore." (It seems groups of Africans patrolled the shore to seize slavers and thereby thwart their voyage.)

By the time Captain Gouget prepared the *Industry* to depart for Jamaica in 1783, three Africans seized the vessel and held it long enough for 103 of the 106 Africans who had been purchased in Goree to disembark "in the old World." (Because the number of Africans who disembarked is three short of the number who boarded, it seems the leaders of the insurrection lost their lives.)

A riveting account of the revolt on the *Amistad* is found in Barbara Chase-Riboud's 1988 historical novel

*Echo of Lions,* from which Steven Spielberg may have adapted the movie in 1997. The uprising was led by Singbe Pieh, a Mendi chief's son who was captured in 1839 and sold to a Spanish slave trader.[6] Commonly called Joseph Cinque, Pieh used a nail he found on the deck of the *Amistad* to release the shackles of fifty-two Africans who were being transported to work on sugar plantations in Principe, Cuba. The men found the weapons on board, killed the captain and the cook, and ordered the crew to sail back to Africa.

The sailors deceived the Africans by sailing north and west at night, eventually reaching Long Island, New York, where the ship was intercepted by United States Navy personnel. Finding the *Amistad* controlled by Africans who had killed two people, the officers took charge and towed the vessel to Connecticut. Some of the Africans were held in Newport; others were transported to Hartford and charged with piracy, loss of property, and murder. Although the charge of murder was dismissed, and the Africans were found not guilty of piracy and loss of property, President Martin Van Buren (1782–1862) orchestrated an appeal of the case to the Supreme Court—a move that brought our sixth president John Quincy Adams (1767–1848) out of his thirty-year retirement to represent the Africans.

Having never owned slaves, President Adams based his defense on the Africans' inherent right to freedom and on the separation of powers mandated by the Constitution: the division of our government into the executive, legislative, and judicial branches, with each branch restricted to its functions only. President

Adams argued that as head of the executive branch, Van Buren had neither the authority to appeal the case nor the right to use his position to influence or interfere with judicial proceedings. Agreeing with Adams, the Supreme Court upheld the not guilty verdict.

With gratitude for their sympathizers' emotional and financial support, Cinque and his friends returned to Sierra Leone in 1842, three years after they were captured.

While the Africans on the *Amistad* survived the Middle Passage and reclaimed their freedom, those on the *Zong* were not so fortunate. In a chilling incident known as the *Zong Massacre,* 132 Africans were murdered.[7] Packed with 470 people and piloted by an inexperienced captain, the *Zong* departed from Africa on September 6, 1781. The overcrowded ship was a breeding ground for disease-bearing bacteria and viruses. In late November, several of the Africans became ill and sixty died, along with seven of the seventeen crew members. The captain made matters worse by sailing past the designated port, the British colony of Jamaica. To cover up his mistake, he ordered the crew to throw some of the sick Africans overboard.

One may question why the captain would do that when he could have sold the men. Well, if the Africans died on board, the captain and crew would be held accountable. If the men died at sea, insurance would cover the loss: in cases of extreme danger, maritime law allows a captain to jettison some of a ship's cargo to lighten the ship.

Because the Africans were considered cargo, those tossed overboard would be documented as "cargo lost at sea," for which the ship's owner could file a claim. His reimbursement from the insurance carrier would have been a lot more than any amount the captain would have received for selling emaciated Africans.

Although the logbook showed the ship had 420 gallons of water when it docked in Jamaica, the owner filed a claim, citing an inadequate amount of water to sustain both the crew and the Africans. The insurer denied the claim, the *Zong's* owner sued, and the Jamaican court ruled in his favor. Public outrage over the ruling moved the highest judge in England, William Murray, First Earl of Mansfield, to order and preside over a second trial. Noting the amount of water listed in the ship's inventory and the captain's navigational errors, judge Murray found in favor of the insurance company. However, because one cannot be tried for murdering cargo, not a single member of the *Zong's* crew was prosecuted.

While the number of Africans killed on the *Zong* is known, no one knows how many men, women, and children Africa lost during the Muslim-Arabs' monopoly of the African slave market from the seventh to the fifteenth centuries. Nor is there a record of the number who died during kidnapping expeditions, those who perished as they shuffled from Africa's inland to ports on its west coast, the number who expired while waiting to board slavers, or the total who succumbed while being broken in at slave ports in the Americas.

UPON THEIR ARRIVAL on American soil, the Africans were taken to a facility, such as a warehouse, to be examined and held until they were deemed free of contagious diseases. To reduce the risk of revolts, workers at the facility separated the Africans: dividing families, Africans who spoke the same language, and those from the same area. When declared disease-free, the Africans were sent to orientation, a euphemism for "breaking" or "seasoning," where they were trained like horses with whips and prods. Poked, prodded, and given morsels of strange food, the Africans were whipped when they did not follow orders given in a language they did not understand. Then, they were taken to slave markets, displayed, and sold, separately of course.

From the slave market, probably more broken-hearted than broken-in, the Africans were transported to farms and plantations, stripped of their names and languages, and forced to work without compensation in rice paddies and cotton fields, on tobacco plantations, in forests and lumber yards, in barns and stables, and in slaveholders' homes, where they cleaned the house, cooked and served the meals, and took care of children too. Some women even nursed their slaveholder's babies, practically rearing many of them, while leaving their own youngsters to the care of older African females who could no longer do heavy manual labor.

Thus began the Africans' lives in America. Like they willed themselves to survive the Middle Passage, they would do the same on land, while keeping their eyes on freedom.

## ♫ Accompaniments ♫

*"Lord, How Come Me Here" surely could have been the mournful cry of African mothers as their children were taken away. Kathleen Battle's rendition of this Negro spiritual is one of the best. "Music Is My Ammunition" sounds like the anguish I imagine the Africans felt on the Middle Passage and as they went through orientation. The heartache*

*they must have felt is sung hauntingly by Playing for Change. The Soweto Gospel Choir captures their yearning for a "World in Union." The choir's rendition of "Africa" appears to speak of life before the continent was ravaged by Arab and European slave traders.*

*Unfortunately, as previously mentioned, the advent of the 366-year Transatlantic slave trade initiated a steady decline in Mali's status as a world power—a downward spiral that affected the entire continent as European colonization grew and 12.5 million of Africa's best were transported to the Americas.8*

*It seems the first twenty Africans who landed in the area known as Jamestown, Virginia, in 1619, may have been indentured servants. By one report, they were traded to the governor for food.9 The textbook for my American History class in college simply described them as "servants." Certainly, they were not slaves because institutionalized slavery had not yet begun in the colonies, and the concept of race was more than a century in the future. I should note here that the first Africans to arrive in the Americas were those who accompanied Spanish explorers in the early 1500s. Some historians identify Pedro Alonzo Niño, one of Columbus's pilots, as the first, followed by 30 Africans who accompanied Vasco Nuñez de Balboa (1475–1519) on the expedition that led to his discovery of the Pacific Ocean in 1513.10 And, around 1538, Esteban Dorantes (1500–1539), held as either a slave or a servant by captain Andrès Dorantes de Carranza, led a group of Spanish explorers into the area known as the states of Arizona and New Mexico today. Esteban's life and travels are documented in Robert Goodwin's book* Crossing the Continent.

*Contrary to how slaves were depicted during dinosaur days or what Lamin and his peers may have learned during African American History Month, the African men and women who were brought to our country came from a continent that contributed many firsts to civilization, including the first stringed instrument; smelting iron; domesticating the sheep, cow, and goat; developing trial by jury; and irrigating and rotating crops.11 And in America, enslaved Africans held a variety of skilled and professional positions: blacksmiths, carpenters, chefs, groomsmen, jockeys, masons, midwives, ministers, nurses, surveyors, and seamstresses, to name a few. Benjamin Banneker (1731–?), a free man skilled in astronomy and mathematics, was one of the men who surveyed the land that became Washington, D.C.*

# Moments
## of Joy

*U*ntil Lamin asked the question, I had never considered the possibility of our enslaved ancestors having fun. Except for yearning to know who they were, I found it too distressing to think about their lives as slaves. But seeing a reflection of my feelings in Lamin's body language, I instinctively envisioned our ancestors' moments of joy: playing games with their children, telling stories, singing, dancing, and celebrating Christmas, which for some was their only day off during the year.

Grateful for the gift of music and a voice to sing, Africans sang humorous work songs, inspiring spirituals, and feet-tapping songs that came to be known as the blues. During slavery, just as it is today, where there is rhythmic music, there is usually dance. Because musical instruments were banned in many areas, enslaved Africans used their hands, feet, sticks, and a clothes-washing device called a rub board as accompaniments. While two or three Africans played the instruments, the others danced.

I imagine they had fun doing the juba, a West African jig popularized in the United States by William Henry Lane (1825–c.1852), a freeborn known as "Mr. Juba." Some tap dancing steps are traced to a version of the juba he performed in minstrel shows.[1] In addition to traditional African dances, slaves enjoyed those they created in America, one of which was the cakewalk. So named because the dancers competed for a cake, the dance is said to have come from the posture and footwork of slaves imitating their "masters" doing the minuet, a dance similar to the waltz. Thus, the cakewalk was likely to have been performed in areas where slaves played the banjo, which is similar to the *akonting*. This popular instrument in the Gambia has three strings, a long neck, and a body made from a calabash gourd with goat skin stretched over it.[2] Slaves who played the banjo at their masters' galas may have had experience with the *akonting*.

Dancing certainly would have been fun at weddings, but slave marriages were not legally recognized. It was not unusual for slaveholders to arrange marriages among their slaves by ordering a man and a woman to share a cabin. Because they could not protect their wives from overseers' and slaveholders' abuse, some men deliberately chose women who lived on another plantation, walking miles to see them when time permitted. With their master's permission, African couples who fell in love simply moved into a cabin together or declared themselves husband and wife if they lived on different farms. In some cases, masters held quasi-marriage ceremonies in their own homes for house slaves, with a white or Negro minister officiating, even though the couple did not have a marriage license.

Field slaves exchanged vows in a ceremony known as "jumping the broom." The bride and groom held hands, faced a broom placed at the front door of their cabin, and jumped over it together. Sometimes a broom was held a foot above the ground for the couple to jump over backward, separately. The one who cleared the broom was declared the "boss," with the one who failed to clear it being "bossed." If both cleared the broom, theirs would be a marriage of equals. Jumping across a broom into their new home symbolized the couple's beginning as a family, a moment of joy for the entire community—including house slaves who, after being "married" in the master's home, held their reception on "slave row" and jumped the broom too.

Slave row, also called "the quarters," was the group of slave cabins that made up the enslaved Africans' community. In the quarters, Africans secretly used names of their own choosing instead of the Anglicized ones slaveholders gave them. Within some families, even different surnames were chosen, a practice that has made it difficult for many African Americans to trace their lineage. In public, the current slaveholder's last name was used, but some Africans kept a former slaveholder's surname, especially if he had treated them well, which appears to have been the case with both of my great grandfathers: Boucher Blocker and Emanuel Johnson. More about them later.

IT SEEMS WITTY Africans had fun telling stories, making jokes, and solving riddles. Many of the gems passed down orally are known as Negro folklore. Mother once told us this story about the slave John:

> At bedtime, John often prayed, "Please, Lord, come down here and take me away from this mean ole master. He gets meaner every day. Seem like nothing John do please him. He just so mean and evil. Please, Lord, come and get John."
>
> One night, just as he kneels to pray, there is a knock on the door.
>
> John's wife asks, "Who is it?"
>
> A voice answers, "It's the Lord. I have come to take John out of his misery, away from his mean master."

*"Just a minute," she says. Then, she calls to John, "The Lord is at the door and has come to take you out of your misery."*

*John jumps up, runs to the back door, and whispers, "Tell him to wait just a few more minutes." Then, off he goes, running.*

*His children cry, "Boohoo, the Lord is going to take our daddy away."*

*Their mother tells them, "Y'all stop that crying. Can't nobody catch John when he's running barefoot."*

LIKE STORYTELLERS HAD fun, so did enslaved Africans who used their wit in court, which, though fraught with risk, resulted in moments of joy.

One such example is Sojourner Truth (c.1797–1883) who sued the people who sold her five-year-old son to a slaveholder in the South. She won that suit as well as the one she filed against a white couple for defamation of character. Her judgment of $125 for the latter was unusual, not only for a Negro but also for a woman.[3] More about her soon.

Although the life of a slave did not lend itself to fun, I imagine gardeners enjoyed the scenery created by the seeds they sowed; seamstresses might have smiled when fabrics they cut and sewed were transformed into comfortable frocks and elegant gowns; musicians would have had fun composing humorous work songs, and those who played the banjo would have had a ball strumming the instrument while "attending" their masters' galas. The Negro folklore I heard in my youth certainly gave me moments of joy.

## ♫ Accompaniments ♫

*Listening to the Soweto Choir's medley, "This Little Light of Mine," / "If You Ever Needed the Lord Before," is like seeing quartets of Africans harmonizing along the quarters on Christmas and New Year's Day. They keep time by chanting, clapping their hands, stamping their feet, or beating sticks. Their concert finished, the singers take turns doing the "Hambone," a game in which players sing as they accompany themselves with sounds made by slaps on the chest and thigh. In my family, two of my brothers would slap themselves from the head to the feet, going all over their body to represent going around the world and back again.*

### HAMBONE

*Hambone, Hambone, where you been?*
*'Round the world and back again!*
*Hambone, Hambone, where's your wife?*
*In the kitchen cooking rice.*
*Hambone, Hambone, have you heard?*
*Papa's gonna buy me a mockingbird.*
*If that mockingbird don't sing,*
*Papa's gonna buy me a diamond ring.*
*If that diamond ring don't shine,*
*Papa's gonna buy me a fishing line.*
*Hambone, Hambone, where you been?*
*'Round the world and back again.*[3]

*The limbo is another game of clapping and motion. From oral history passed down by their African ancestors, melanin-rich people in Trinidad created the limbo, a popular line dance that symbolizes the descent to the hold. Going down the ship's stairwell, Africans had to lean back so far their heads almost touched the steps.*

*The lyrics suggest "Sitting in Limbo" was composed in the 1950s when Trinidad and Tobago joined forces to gain their independence from Great Britain. The islands were in limbo until England honored their demand for self-government on August 31, 1962, after which they adopted the name Tri-nidad-Tobago. Jimmy Cliff's reggae rendition of this song may be more appealing to Lamin and other readers with Jamaican roots. Jamaica's independence preceded Trinidad's by three weeks, on August 6, 1962. I can see Lamin raising his fist and exclaiming, "It's All Right!"*

# Adapting and Escaping

Separated from everyone they knew, speaking a different language than their new acquaintances, and lacking the means to return to the motherland, Africans could either accept their condition, adapt to it, or escape to areas where slavery was not allowed. Although unfamiliar with their surroundings, some Africans did attempt to escape, but not knowing where to run for freedom, they were soon captured, labeled "runaways," and returned to their "masters."

Taking advantage of the Africans' compromised situation, Europeans who settled in the thirteen colonies that became the United States sought to keep the slaves in bondage. Thinking illiteracy would ensure the permanency of slavery, some of them passed laws making it a crime to teach slaves to read and write. Anyone caught doing so was subject to imprisonment or public flogging, probably in the town square. Consequently, there were no schools for enslaved Africans.

Given only on-the-job training, Africans adapted by memorizing almost everything they heard and saw: conversations, especially those about free states and legal matters; Scripture cited in sermons; local geography such as trails, streams, and rivers; and landmarks like buildings, caves, trees, and shrubs, noting their locations, sizes, and shapes. Like they had done in their native land, Africans also identified edible and inedible plants as well as constellations. Those who escaped used stars, particularly the North Star, as well as local landmarks as guides and edible plants as food.

Having learned to do their jobs by memorizing, Africans learned to assess character by scrutinizing the demeanor of each individual who had a role in controlling their lives: slave-holders, overseers, merchants, children, and even other slaves, especially house slaves who may have been taught to read well enough to carry out their duties, and also those who secretly learned to read by listening to their master's children while they were being taught, by asking them questions, or even by allowing the children to teach them. As you might imagine, trustworthy servants were a valuable resource for Africans who were planning to escape.

Slaves thought to be overly servile to whites were kept at a distance, with males eventually labeled "Uncle Toms," after the main character in Harriett Beecher Stowe's novel *Uncle Tom's Cabin*—a book said to have brought one or two pro-slavers to tears while shifting hundreds of abolitionists into high gear. But the pejorative "Uncle Tom" was not always warranted. Possibly more often than not, Africans who acted subservient merely did so to disguise their feelings. Based on their knowl-edge of an individual's character, they tailored their actions to appease or cajole, rather than risk provoking or creating suspi-cions with an uncontrolled facial expression or an uncensored verbal response.

In 1896, Paul Laurence Dunbar (1872–?) wrote a poem about this guise.

WE WEAR THE MASK

*We wear the mask that grins and lies,*
*It hides our cheeks and shades our eyes –*
*This debt we pay to human guile:*
*With torn and bleeding hearts we smile,*
*And mouth with myriad subtleties.*

*Why should the world be over-wise,*
*In counting all our tears and sighs?*
*Nay, let them only see us, while*
*We wear the mask.*

*We smile, but, O great Christ, our cries*
*To thee from tortured souls arise,*
*We sing, but oh the clay is vile*
*Beneath our feet, and long the mile:*
*But let the world dream otherwise,*
*We wear the mask!*

The mask was and still is a way of coping, which we all do at times. But to maintain some semblance of autonomy, enslaved Africans made the mask a way of life, along with secret modes of communication.

Not allowed to speak in their native tongue or to meet in groups without the presence of an overseer or slaveholder, the Africans sent messages by drums. When their secret was discovered, however, South Carolina passed laws prohibiting the use of drums, and Georgia made it illegal for slaves to play drums, horns, or any loud instruments. The Africans adapted by using words with double meanings in conversations and in songs, of which the most notable came to be known as Negro spirituals.

Based on Scripture, the earliest spirituals were composed by unknown slaves who, more than likely, could not read or write, and as non-citizens could not copyright their compositions. Enslaved Africans memorized the songs and sang specific spirituals as a means of mass communication. For example, the hymns "There Is a Balm in Gilead" and "Fix Me Jesus" had sacred as well as secular meanings.

In Scripture, balm is an oil with healing properties, and Gilead is an area known for producing the most effective curative oils. Hence, to the slaves, "balm" might have symbolized the healing of an injury or freedom, and "Gilead" could have signified Canada or any free state. In its sacred context, fix means forgive, but to a slave, fix could have meant prepare, as in make ready to escape; or it could have been translated as comfort for a loss or respite from the pain of an injury.


SLAVES WHO FAILED in their attempt to escape were severely punished. In addition to beatings with a whip, punishments included what was known as "mild maiming," such as cutting the Achilles tendon or amputating an ear, a finger, or a toe. Injuring the foot left the slave able to work but unable to outrun patrollers, men hired to capture missing slaves. A slave without an ear was easily identified as a troublemaker and thereby subject to more scrutiny, which made it almost impossible to attempt another escape.

Considered as property, slaves who did escape "stole" themselves from their slaveholders. When an individual sang "Steal Away," he was either covertly announcing a meeting that slaves should "steal away" to, or he was conveying his plan to escape during the next thunderstorm. Thus, bloodhounds could not track him because rain would wash away his footprints and odors.

## STEAL AWAY

*Steal away, steal away, steal away to Jesus.*
*Steal away, steal away home.*
*I ain't got long to stay here.*
*My Lord calls me,*
*He calls me by the thunder,*
*The trumpet sounds within my soul,*
*I ain't got long to stay here.*
*Steal away, steal away, steal away to Jesus.*
*Steal away, steal away home.*
*I ain't got long to stay here.*

Masking plans to escape with a song was brilliant. The Africans believed that like God sent Moses to lead the enslaved Hebrews to freedom, He would send someone to guide them too. Singing "Swing Low, Sweet Chariot" or "Go Down Moses" sent the message that their "Moses" was somewhere in the area. "Chariot" and "Moses" were codes for Harriett Tubman (c.1820–1913).

Tubman escaped by walking ninety miles from Maryland to Pennsylvania. She returned to the South nineteen times to help over 300 slaves escape, including her seventy-year-old parents. Like slaves who sang "If You Don't Go, Don't Hinder Me" when cautioned by others, Tubman may have spoken those same words to her husband, who dallied over running away but ultimately chose to stay put.

Taking the position that dead slaves do not talk, Tubman carried a gun. If a runaway became tired or frightened and attempted to return to his owner, she aimed her gun and said, "Live North or die here."[1] She could not risk having the strategies of her covert operation or the identity of her agents exposed.

Tubman's agents were known as conductors on the Underground Railroad, a secret network of resources for enslaved Africans who were escaping to free states, Canada, Mexico, and areas such as Kansas and Oklahoma, where slavery was not common. Resources included hidden trails and safe shelters known as depots or stations. Conductors provided clothing, food, and lodging for runaways as well as transportation or directions to the next depot or station.

Stations may have been a freedman's home or a house owned by a member of the Religious Society of Friends. Called Quakers by non-members, Friends were among the British immigrants who came to America to escape religious persecution. Traveling in wagons with camouflaged compartments, Friends transported Tubman's passengers from one depot to the next. A "depot" might have been a home that had a room with a trapdoor. This door opened to a cellar or an attic where enough supplies were stored to sustain a runaway until he or she could go to the next station—usually a freedman's home, or any place deemed safe such as a stable, barn, church, woodshed, or abandoned cabin.

OF ENSLAVED AFRICANS' four options—accepting slavery, adapting to it, fleeing from it, or buying themselves—more emphasis was placed on the first two during dinosaur days. Concerned that Lamin may have had a similar experience at school, I focused on the last two to fully answer his question.

Of course, most slaves did adapt, but thousands fled, and thousands more purchased their own freedom and that of family members too. Those who bought freedom did so by saving the portion of their earnings the slaveholder allowed them to keep when he hired them out to other plantation owners—either as field hands or skilled craftsmen such as carpenters, cooks, blacksmiths, painters, and seamstresses.

Unfortunately, time and space limit the number of stories I can share about the numerous individuals who chose not to accept or adapt to slavery. Allow me to begin with two men who may have been the most instrumental in facilitating escapes and reuniting family members, respectively.

A couple with strong convictions, Levi Coffin (1798–1877) and his wife may have helped the most runaways.[2] Members of the Religious Society of Friends, they placed their moral obligation to aid runaways above the law, specifically the Fugitive Slave Act of 1793, which gave slaveholders the right to capture and re-enslave runaways. Thus, the couple moved from North Carolina to Newport, Indiana, where along with shelter and food, they kept a supply of new clothes for fugitives, courtesy of Quaker women who met at their home to make the garments. During their twenty years in Newport, the Coffins helped over 2,000 Africans escape, mostly to Canada.

In 1847, Coffin moved to Cincinnati and established a business that sold only products produced by free laborers. It is estimated he helped another 1,000 runaways in Cincinnati. Fondly dubbed "the president of the Underground Railroad," Coffin was a true friend.[3]

∝⌇

Though he was not a Quaker, William Still (1821–1902), called "Father of the Underground Railroad," was the friend runaways sought in Philadelphia, Pennsylvania. The youngest of sixteen children, Still kept notes on fugitive slaves to help new escapees locate and reunite with family members. Through his work, his own family was reunited.

Still's father, Levin, moved from Maryland to New Jersey after purchasing his own freedom in 1798. Still's mother Sydney was captured on her first attempt to run away with the couple's four children, but she succeeded the second time by taking only her two younger daughters. After she joined her husband in New Jersey, the couple had fourteen more children. Their two eldest, Peter and Levin, were the ones Sydney left behind. While the six- and five-year-old lads sat on the porch waiting for her to return, a slave trader captured the boys, took them to Kentucky, and sold them. Levin died a slave in Alabama, but Peter, at the age of forty-eight—with help from the Jewish Friedman brothers—purchased his freedom. He then went to search for his mother, leaving his wife and three children in Tuscumbia, Alabama.

When he arrived in Philadelphia, conductors directed him to William Still's office. Hearing Peter's story, Still knew he was listening to one of his own brothers their mother had left behind but had never forgotten. The emotional mother and son reunion that was forty-two years in the making is beautifully told in *The Kidnapped and the Ransomed* by Kate E.R. Pickard, first published in 1856.

From a novel letter-writing campaign, Peter raised

enough money to pay the $5,000 asking price for his family. In 1856, his wife and children arrived in Cincinnati. They made Levi Coffin's home their first stop.

∞

Still's office was also the destination of one of the Underground Railroad's most desperate but daring runaways, Henry Brown (1815–1897).[4] Brown lived in Richmond, Virginia, where he worked in his master's tobacco factory; his wife and children lived on an adjacent plantation. When his pregnant wife and their three children were sold to a slave owner in North Carolina, Brown could take no more.

Upon hearing about an abolitionist who accepted runaways as freight, Brown had himself shipped to Philadelphia. He climbed into a box and lay in a fetal position while two friends cut a hole in the box for air, nailed it, and tied it with straps. Brown lay in the box for twenty-seven hours until he was delivered to William Still at the Philadelphia Anti-Slavery Society on March 25, 1849.

Soon thereafter, "Henry Box Brown," as he came to be known, launched his career on the lecture circuit, recounting his escape and advocating the abolition of slavery. But passage of the Fugitive Slave Act on August 30, 1850, forced him to place his act on hold and immigrate to England in October 1850. He returned to the states with a new wife in 1875.

Josiah Henson (1789–1883) fled from slavery with his wife and four children in 1830. A young boy when purchased by Isaac Riley, Henson became a minister in the African Methodist Episcopal Church. With his eye on freedom, he saved his earnings and made a $350 down payment toward Riley's $450 asking price. In financial straits himself, Riley took Henson's down payment with a promise to send the manumission—slavery release—papers to his brother Amos who had agreed to keep his slaves temporarily. A trusting and loyal man, Henson carried the letter as he led the group of slaves to Amos's plantation. Unbeknownst to him, Riley had broken his promise: the letter showed $1,000 as the purchase price, with instructions to sell Henson.

While he was transporting Henson to the New Orleans slave market, Amos's son became ill. Ever loyal, Henson nursed the young man back to health and brought him home. But after his good deed went unacknowledged, Henson bade loyalty farewell, took his wife and children, and walked from Kentucky to Ohio.

Aided by Native Americans and white sympathizers, the Hensons made their way to Buffalo, New York, and eventually to Canada. There, Henson became a successful farmer while continuing his ministry, sharing his knack for farming with other African immigrants and spearheading the community's efforts to become economically independent.

Although some historians have questioned the authenticity of Harriet Jacobs' (1813–1897) autobiography, I am fascinated by her story of self-liberation. When her mother died, six-year-old Harriet became the property of Margaret Horniblow. Horniblow taught Harriet to read, write, and sew; but she willed her to a six-year-old niece whose father became Harriett's crude master.

Thinking she could avoid the man's advances and liberate herself too, Jacobs accepted the friendship of his neighbor, Samuel Tredwell Sawyer—a friendship that led to his fathering her two children. Children born to slaves were owned by their parents' slaveholder. So, gambling on Sawyer's buying and freeing the children, Jacobs fled when her master became her "legal owner." After rebuffing him for years, she did not protest when he ordered her to move into the "big house"—even bringing her own mattress as instructed. But, she never slept on it. As soon as the sounds of sleep from the master bedroom filled the house, Jacobs quietly stole away her first night there. With the help of friends and relatives, she hid in a benevolent white woman's concealed attic until she could be safely escorted—disguised as a dark-skinned male—to her grandmother Molly's home.

Freed in 1828, Molly (last name unknown) had remained in Edenton, North Carolina, to be near her family. Jacobs spent seven years hidden in the crawl space of a small shed that was attached to Molly's house. There, she read the Bible, sewed, and periodically looked through a peephole to watch her children play in the yard. Taking the Underground Railroad, Jacobs made New York her last stop. She rejected the notion of humans as property and refused supporters' offers to purchase her freedom. However, her employer's wife paid Harriett's former slaveholder $300 to prevent him from re-enslaving her per the Fugitive Slave Act of 1850.

∞

Self-reliance and creativity also marked George and Ellen Craft's escape from Georgia. Often mistaken for a member of her slaveholder's family, Ellen (1826–1891) was a fair-complexioned house servant. Her dark-skinned husband William (1824–1900), a cabinetmaker, saved a portion of his earnings and secretly bought supplies for their getaway: Ellen would be disguised as a sick white man, traveling with his servant, William.[5]

To leave their slaveholder's premises without a written pass, enslaved Africans risked being captured and sold. Ellen and William secured passes to leave on December 21, 1848, a cover to prevent their stay beyond Christmas from becoming suspicious.

William cut Ellen's hair, then gave her a man's jacket, a pair of green glasses, a scarf for her beardless face, and a sling for her right arm. Ellen wore the jacket with the men's trousers she had made, capping her outfit off with a top hat.

They told curious travelers that the scarf alleviated a toothache, and the sling protected a broken wrist. Actually, keeping her hand in the sling concealed Ellen's inability to read and write, which rendered her unable to sign in at hotels that accommodated them in Charleston, Richmond, and Baltimore.

Three weeks after their arrival in Philadelphia, upon the advice of Underground Railroad conductors, they continued on to Boston. Although William found work as a cabinetmaker and Ellen as a seamstress, they immigrated to England when a warrant for their arrest was issued per the Fugitive Slave Law in the Compromise of 1850. After twenty years in England, the Crafts returned to America and in the 1870s established a school for Negroes in Georgia.

While the Compromise of 1850 forced the Crafts to emigrate, a loophole was instrumental in freeing Jane Johnson (1814–1872). The law required the capture and return of slaves who escaped to free states, but it did not address slaves whose owners *brought* them to a free state.

In the summer of 1855, slaveholder John Wheeler (1806–1882) brought Johnson and her children with him and his family from Washington, D.C., to Philadelphia. After visiting relatives there, he planned to take a ferry to New York, where he would board a ship to Nicaragua, his post as United States Minister.

Under Pennsylvania law, slaveholders had no property rights over slaves if they voluntarily brought them into the state. It seems both Wheeler and Johnson were aware of the law and of Philadelphia's large freedmen population, 11 percent. Wheeler told Johnson not to talk to anyone in the city or to say she was free, but Johnson paid him no never-mind. She expressed her wish for freedom first with a colored woman and later with a colored man. One of them scribbled out a note about Johnson's situation and handed it to a child conductor for delivery to William Still's office. Still then contacted Passmore Williamson (1822–1895), a white abolitionist who was also a Quaker Underground Railroad conductor.

The two men put on their detective caps and had a few missteps, but arrived at the harbor before the ferry left. Spotting Wheeler's party on an upper deck, Still shouted to Johnson, told her she was free, and urged her to disembark. When she attempted to leave, Wheeler stepped in her way. But Williamson detained him while Still and five colored dockworkers escorted Johnson and her children to a depot.

Wheeler sued Still and the dockworkers for assault and battery. Then, at his request, a judge summoned Williamson to bring Johnson and her children to court. Because conductors knew only the details of their individual assignments, Williamson had no idea where Johnson was. Thus, when he came to court alone, he was imprisoned for "contempt."

Out of the blue, Johnson appeared at Still's trial and testified she had chosen to be free. Still and three of the dockworkers were acquitted; the other two were fined $10 and sentenced to one week in jail. Williamson was released after three months; Johnson and her children lived freely ever after, as did her replacement Hannah Bond (c.1830s?–c.1880s?).

∝

A house slave for the Wheelers, Hannah Bond is thought to have been born in Virginia and sold multiple times—perhaps the first being from the plantation where an elderly white couple who lived nearby ran afoul of the law for teaching her to read and write. It seems Bond's thirst for knowledge was second to her desire for freedom, followed by her stance against slave marriages, which she saw as a tool for perpetuating slavery.

Bond cringed at life in slave quarters, and she vowed to escape rather than share a cabin with anyone. She kept the vow when Wheeler's wife demoted her and offered her in marriage to a field slave. At nightfall, after her first day in the field, Bond escaped disguised as a man. It is speculated that Wheeler's sympathetic nephew supplied the suit she wore.

After fleeing from Murfreesboro, North Carolina, Bond was guided by Underground Railroad conductors to New York. Given refuge by the Craft family, she lived on their farm before moving to New Jersey, where she became a teacher and married a minister.

Considering Bond's disguise, she either took William and Ellen Crafts' surname or that of the Craft family in New York when she wrote her autobiographical novel. Written in 1857, the book is the earliest known one written by an African American woman. However, *Our Nig*, by freewoman Harriet E. Wilson, was the first novel written by a black female to be published (1859). Two notes here:

- According to "Professor Says He Has Solved a Mystery Over a Slave's Novel," an article that appeared in the *New York Times* September 18, 2013, Dorothy Porter Wesley (1905–1995) purchased Craft's manuscript from a New York City bookseller for $85 in 1948.

- By having a friend bid $8,500 at an auction, the only bid submitted, renowned historian Henry Louis Gates secured the handwritten manuscript in 2001. Published in 2002, *The Bondwoman's Narrative* became a *New York Times* bestseller.

While a bit different from Bond's case, marriage was the determining factor for Jenny Slew (c.1719–?). Because her free white mother was married to an enslaved African, Slew lived as a free woman until she was kidnapped and enslaved in 1762. The Massachusetts Bay Colony allowed slaves to file civil suits, so Jenny engaged a lawyer to sue for her freedom in 1765. The court ruled in the slaveholder's favor: Jenny's husband was not party to the suit, and as a married woman, she could not sue on her own behalf.

But Jenny had an ace. Although she had been married a few times, each spouse was a slave, and marriage between slaves was not considered legal. Back to court Jenny went. Thus, based on her mother's status, a jury in Salem, Massachusetts, awarded her four pounds in damages and set her free in 1766.

Elizabeth Freeman, known as Mum Bett (1742–1829), received her freedom and similar damages in 1780: thirty shillings and court costs. Overhearing conversations about the Bill of Rights and Massachusetts' new constitution, Freeman determined that she, too, was born free and equal.

Subsequently, after receiving a blow with a hot kitchen shovel aimed at her sister, Bett fled from the estate of her slaveholder, John Ashley. She then hired attorney Theodore Sedgwick to sue Ashley for her freedom. After winning her case, Freeman rejected Ashley's offer of a salaried position. Instead, she worked as the Sedgwicks' housekeeper until she established her own business as a midwife and nurse.

♨

In 1841, fugitive Madison Washington (c.1819–?) was recaptured when he returned from Canada to Virginia for his wife. Placed on the *Creole* with 134 Africans who were being transported from Virginia to the New Orleans' slave market—with one escape to his credit—he was not about to be re-enslaved. On November 7, Washington bolted from the hold after a crew member lifted the gate. Eighteen men followed him. With only a knife, they took control of the vessel, sparing the overseer's life in exchange for his sailing the ship to the British West Indies.

Despite slaveholders' protests, their ensuing lawsuits, and the United States's demand for the slaves' return, the men were declared free under British colonial law, which abolished slavery in 1834. The slaveholders' suit lingered for fifteen years, during which time the leaders of the revolts were exonerated and many of their accomplices sailed to Jamaica, courtesy of the government in Nassau. Finally, rather than subject the United States to war, Great Britain paid the slaveholders for loss of property: $20,000 for each slave in today's money.

The *Creole* Rebellion freed the most Africans—128 —than any single slave revolt in our country's history. By some reports, 100,000 slaves were freed via the Underground Railroad, many from the 700 depots in Ohio, including Oberlin College, one of the first to admit Negro students.

Although strategically located and a free state as of 1802, Ohio passed the first "Black Laws" in 1804. Designed to limit the civil rights of free African residents, the laws discouraged slaves from entering the state, made sheltering runaways illegal, ordered whites to report fugitives, and compensated those who did. Runaways ignored the codes, endured unimaginable conditions, and accepted all kinds of risks to take a ferry from Cincinnati to Canada. Canada did not return runaways to our country, so risks such as hypothermia, starvation, and recapture were well worth taking. About 40,000 slaves escaped to Canada via depots in Ohio, thirteen of which are now historical sites.

According to "Explore Canadian Stops on the Underground Railroad," an article in the September 15,

2013, issue of the *Detroit Free Press*, 30,000 slaves fled to Ontario, Canada, between 1834 and 1860 by way of depots in Detroit, Michigan. The article pays homage to the Underground Railroad and its historic sites in Ontario, Canada, with a special note on John and Jane Freeman Walls. In 1846, the interracial couple took the Underground Railroad from Troublesome Creek in Rockingham, North Carolina, to Amhertsburg, Ontario, Canada.

John (1813–1909) and his slaveholder's son Daniel Walls were born on the same day. Both were nursed by John's mother whose husband Hannibal was shot and killed when he tried to escape. Subsequently, the murderer, Daniel's father Eli Walls, kept fifteen-year-old John but sold the lad's mother Jubil. Eventually, Daniel took over the plantation's operations and promoted John to overseer.

After marrying Jane King (1822–1910) and fathering four children, Daniel succumbed to a grave illness in 1845. On his deathbed, he freed John and asked him to take care of Jane and the children. Though John and Jane grew to love each other, Jane knew that Daniel's relatives would prevent her and John from inheriting the plantation, one of the wealthiest in the area. What's more, North Carolina certainly would not issue them a marriage license. Leaving the state was their only option.

Traveling with four children, the couple could not have survived without the help of Native Americans and Quaker abolitionists. Guided along the Underground Railroad by Quaker conductors, John and Jane married in Indiana before continuing to Canada. The home John built in Lakeshore, Ontario, is now the Walls Historic Site.

∞

Clara Brown was born in Virginia and sold several times, even away from her husband and four children. In 1859, she persuaded a group of prospectors to hire her as a cook on their wagon train to Denver, where she had heard her daughter Eliza lived. Not finding Eliza in Denver, Brown moved on to Central City, opened a laundry, served as a nurse and midwife, and invested in gold mines, amassing a $10,000 fortune by 1866—more than enough to search for her family. Although her daughter was the only immediate family member she reunited with, Brown did locate thirty-four relatives whom she brought to Denver.

Not all escapes, however, resulted in happy endings.

On a cold January night, the Garner party walked across the frozen Ohio River from Kentucky to Cincinnati, the first stop on their way to Canada. Arriving in broad daylight and attempting to avoid attracting attention, Robert (?–1871), Margaret (1834–1858), their four children, and his parents split up from their traveling companions, who were slaves from another plantation. Conductors escorted the other slaves to various depots until they made their way to Canada.

After the group separated, local residents became suspicious when they overheard the Garners asking for directions to Elijah Kite's home, a freedman. As a result, when Elijah left the family at his house to seek a safer depot, slaveholder Archibald K. Gaines and a posse of federal marshals arrived to arrest them.

Finding the Garners barricaded inside the house and refusing to answer, the officers knocked down the door. Robert shot and seriously wounded one of the officers before he himself was attacked. Desperate for freedom at any cost, Margaret killed one of the couple's four children and attempted to kill the others and herself.

During an interview, Margaret said she would have killed all her children to free them from the horrors of slavery.[6] Ultimately, the Garners were re-enslaved.

A soldier in his father's army, Prince Abdul Rahman Ibrahim (c.1762–1829) was captured during a battle around 1788. He was subsequently sold to British slave traders who shipped him to the Dominican Republic. From there, he was transferred to New Orleans, Louisiana, and from New Orleans to Natchez, Mississippi, where he was bought by slaveholder Thomas Foster.[7]

Although impressed by Abdul's intelligence and carriage, Foster did not believe he was a prince. Unable to convince Foster his father would pay whatever ransom requested, Adbul initially refused to do any manual labor and instead made several attempts to escape. In time, he adapted, married, and became a trustworthy servant, growing vegetables in the garden Foster gave him.

One day, while selling potatoes at the market, Prince Abdul saw a white man who looked familiar. When the man, Dr. Cox, approached Abdul, both men recognized each other. Cox, a recent Irish immigrant, was a surgeon on a ship before he moved to America. On a trip to Africa, he went ashore, lost his way, and became disoriented. When he finally came back to the dock, he found the ship had left without him. A group of boys saw Cox, ran to the king—Prince Abdul's father—and told him they had seen a white man. The king instructed the boys to bring the man to his home. Upon discovering Cox had a sore leg, the king arranged for a woman to treat it. Pleased with his medical care and the king's hospitality, Cox lived with Prince Abdul's family for over six months.

Hoping to free the man who was a boy when they first met, Cox assured Foster that Abdul was indeed a prince and offered large sums to purchase him.[8] Having come to rely on Abdul's agricultural expertise and on his skills in managing livestock and supervising the other slaves, Foster refused the offers. Although relentless, Cox died before he could free Abdul. Sometime after the prince's story appeared in major newspapers, Foster accepted the substantial sum Cox's son offered for Abdul and later agreed to sell his wife. Contributions from sympathizers enabled the couple to move to Liberia, where Abdul died five months later.

ALTHOUGH SCORES OF Africans chose to "purchase" themselves, that choice had limitations too. Called "freedmen" after buying their freedom, they were not entirely free. The term freedmen simply meant slaveholders could no longer claim the Africans as property. Freedmen were not citizens, could not vote, and could be re-enslaved if found guilty of any "crime," such as not moving off the walkway for a white person, not having a job, or the catch-all crime of insolence: a look, walk, or response a white considered "uppity."

Despite their precarious position, freedmen and "freed-women" were represented in most states, including those in the South. As a matter of fact, according to the 1850 census, there were over 109,000 "free colored" in seven southern states, including 898 in Mississippi.

Although some mulattoes—biracial slaves—were shunned and even sold by their white parent, it seems they comprised the majority of freedmen, a result of having been set free upon the death of their slaveholders, who in some cases were the slaves' own fathers. Of course, a few mulattoes had white mothers, but most of those women lost not only their slaves but also their status and inheritance when their liaisons were exposed. Thus men and women who were freed by their slave-holding fathers were more likely to have been trained in a trade and given money or property so they could establish a business, purchase more land, or even buy slaves.

William Johnson (1809–1851), a mulatto who lived in Natchez, Mississippi, did all three. At the age of eleven, Johnson was freed by slaveholder William Johnson, who is thought to have been his father. Trained as a barber, Johnson built a successful business that enabled him to purchase land and slaves; he owned sixteen when he died in 1851. In 1990, the city of Natchez donated Johnson's house to the National Park Service, which opened the home as a museum in 2005.

Unlike Johnson, the mulatto George Washington (1817–1905) never knew his biological father, an enslaved African who was sold and taken away from the area shortly after Washington's birth. Fortunately, however, his white mother gave him to a white couple who migrated westward from Virginia, finally settling in Oregon. With their help, Washington obtained 640 acres of land, some of which he sold in 1875 to grow the town of Centerville, Washington, later changing the name to Centralia. A generous man of many trades —marksman, miller, distiller, tanner, weaver, cook, spinner—Washington helped the needy, donated money to build churches, and did not foreclose on mortgages he held during the Panic of 1893.[9] Thought to be the largest city founded by an African American, Centralia had a population of 16,336 on the 2010 census. Today, approximately 85 percent of the population is white, while about one percent is African American.

Jim Beckwourth, also a mulatto, left the blacksmith apprenticeship his white father arranged for him to become an explorer, fur trader, and mountain man. In 1850, he discovered what is known as the Beckwourth Mountain Pass through the Sierra Nevada Mountains.

He led the first group of settlers through the pass, which is northwest of Reno, Nevada.

∞

Sojourner Truth bought her freedom with labor. When her slaveholder reneged on his promise to free her, she continued to work for him, unpaid, until—by her calculations—she had toiled long enough to cover the cost for her freedom. At that point, in 1828, she simply packed and moved from upstate New York to New York City. She changed her name from Isabella Baumfree to Sojourner—for the itinerant preacher she became—and Truth, because she believed ministers speak the truth.

A proponent for women's rights, Sojourner spoke the truth when she said, "I can't read, but I can hear. I have heard the Bible and have learned that Eve caused man to sin. Well, if woman upset the world, do give her a chance to set it right side up again."[10]

During her time, Truth and many thousands more certainly did their part to turn our country in the right direction. Yes, some had help from white conductors, other freedmen, Native Americans, and Spanish settlers, but most Africans who escaped or purchased their freedom masked their plans, relying only on trusted friends, their own wit, or their hard-won earnings.

## ♫ Accompaniments ♫

✑

*I imagine Harriett Tubman might have shouted "Free at Last" upon arriving in Philadelphia, Pennsylvania. While this song by the Five Blind Boys of Alabama is quite common, I like a similar one from the musical* Big River. *How I wish Tubman could have heard Ron Richardson sing "Muddy Water" and "River in the Rain": she advised runaways to keep close to a stream. Richardson won the 1985 Tony Award for his role in* Big River.

*By conducting her train during the winter and on Saturday nights, Tubman gave her passengers a head start: slaveholders could not advertise missing slaves until the following Monday. She is reported to have said, "I never run my train off the track, and I never lost a passenger."*

*Endowed with vision—an ability that includes creativity, resourcefulness, and steadfastness—enslaved Africans defied the confines of time and place. Vision sustained them on the Middle Passage; beyond bodies bound by chains, they saw liberation and justice. Vision enabled them not only to adapt to their new world in America, but also to escape from its horrors. In Scripture, they saw songs of praise and messages of deliverance. After the Civil War, some Negroes considered the spirituals as reminders of past events best left to rest. Ironically, an unfortunate situation saved the songs.*

*A growing enrollment, especially of students who needed financial aid, brought the school that became Fisk University to the brink of bankruptcy. Hoping to restore the university's fiscal health, the director of music took the newly formed choir on a fund-raising concert tour.*

*White audiences were so moved by the spirituals that the choir, which became known as the Fisk Jubilee Singers, was invited to perform at more venues than expected. Consequently, the tour netted not only enough contributions to prevent Fisk's bankruptcy, it also led the university to collect and preserve the Negro spirituals.*

*Some African American organizations hold an annual Negro Spirituals Concert in February. Usually, the songs are sung a cappella to honor how they were sung originally. However, concert versions have instrumental accompaniments.*

*Although Wallace Willis, a slave who lived in Oklahoma, is said to have composed "Swing Low, Sweet Chariot," I found only two references that identify him as the composer: one online and one on the sleeve of the CD* Freedom Is Coming: Songs of Freedom, Resistance & the Underground Railroad. *Incidentally, the rendition of the spirituals on this CD is one of the best I have heard.*

# Flights and Fights for Freedom

M any privileges Americans enjoy today can be credited to Europeans who largely fled to the thirteen colonies to avoid religious persecution, a practice seen worldwide for hundreds of years.

In western Europe, Catholicism was the major religion until ministers—particularly Martin Luther (1483–1546) and John Calvin (1509–1564)—suggested reforming some of its doctrines. Their protests against practices such as confessing to a priest and purchasing certificates signed by the Pope for the forgiveness of sin gave birth to Protestantism.

In the early 1500s, people who believed faith alone was the means to salvation established their own Protestant churches. However, if their ruler's belief differed, they had to either convert to his or her religion, immigrate to another country, or risk being spied on, tortured, or burned at the stake for heresy. Such was the fate of Spain's Jewish population during the Spanish Inquisition (1478–1834).[1]

Initially an order to prevent heresy, the Inquisition ultimately targeted Jews, forcing some to convert to Catholicism, then spying on them to see if they were secretly practicing Judaism. Upon receiving reports that some converts were indeed observing Jewish customs, Queen Isabella issued an edict on March 31, 1492, ordering all Jews to convert or leave the country by July 31, 1492. Half of the Jews converted, while the rest fled, unable to take anything of value with them.

Similarly, in Italy, Pope Paul III issued the Roman Inquisition in 1542, placing Italians under surveillance. Those found practicing any Protestant religion were tried as heretics. Consequently, Protestantism was eliminated throughout the country, and Catholicism became the official religion of Italy, with the Pope as the ruling authority of the Catholic Church worldwide.

In Great Britain, a change in King Henry VIII's (1491–1547) religion meant a new religion for the people who adopted it and execution for those who did not. Failing to father a male heir with his first wife Catherine, King Henry asked the Pope to annul the marriage. The Pope refused. Somehow, Henry managed to separate the Catholic Church of England from the Roman Catholic Church, and thereby succeeded in having his marriage annulled. After the separation, the Church of England was sometimes referred to—often as it is today—by its denomination, Anglican.

Britons who remained Catholics or adopted a Protestant denomination other than Anglican were tried for heresy, which was also considered treason. King Henry ordered those convicted to be burned at the stake.

Following Henry's lead, King James I (1566–1625) persecuted Britons who chose not to join the Church of England. Rather than risk death or endure harassment for choosing a religion that encompassed their beliefs, Britons immigrated to Germany or Switzerland during the 1500s, and to the Americas in the 1600s and 1700s.

A group of Christians who had separated from the Anglican church were among the 102 passengers who sailed to

"New England" on the *Mayflower*. Known as the Pilgrims, the group landed at Plymouth Rock in 1620, the surrounding area of which became the second permanent British settlement in America—the first being Chesapeake, Virginia, in 1607.[2] Diverse groups of Britons followed—some for freedom of religion, others for economic opportunities, and probably a few for adventure.

After making their homes on land secured from Native Americans by trade, treaties, or warfare, and building an economy based on products produced by enslaved Africans and indentured servants, the immigrants, historically known as colonists, were free to practice a religion of their choice. But, as British subjects, they were still bound by British rules.

With no representatives in England's parliament to protect their interests, the colonists resorted to public demonstrations to express their objections to taxes and laws that restricted free enterprise. For example, in addition to tariffs on coffee and wine, the Sugar Act mandated timber, oil, and a few other products be exported to the mother country only; the Stamp Act required almost all written documents be printed on stamped paper issued and taxed by British agents in the colonies; and the Tea Act exempted the East India Company from paying taxes on tea it sold directly to retailers, but left the tariffs intact for merchants. Considering the exemption as granting a tea monopoly and concerned that other commodities would be exempted too, merchants objected. Rather than continue to pay taxes to a country whose rigid class system denied them the social mobility afforded in the Americas, the men sought to keep their money and manage the colonies as an independent republic.

When attempts to negotiate an amicable separation from the mother country failed, groups of colonists expressed their grievances in the streets. In response, Great Britain ordered the troops stationed in the colonies to quell the demonstrations—which would prove to be a deadly decision.

On the night of March 5, 1770, the troops clashed with a group of Bostonians. Tempers flared and civilians threw rubbish at the soldiers who, in return, fired into a crowd described as "a motley rabble of saucy boys, negroes, mulattoes, Irish teagues, and outlandish Jack tars (sailors).[3] Crispus Attucks (c.1723–1770)—a biracial man said to have had an African father and a Native American mother—was the first of five people killed. Known as the Boston Massacre, this protest was followed by more civil unrest, with civilians demanding the commanding officer be charged with murder. The uproar quieted after John Adams (1735–1826) won the officer's acquittal. Adams, who became the second president of the United States, argued that officer Thomas Preston had only given the order to fire.

Protests flared up again with the passage of the Tea Act in 1773. On December 16, about 100 men disguised themselves as members of the Mohawk Native American Nation, boarded a ship, and threw cargoes of tea into Boston Harbor. (The tea would be worth about a million dollars today.) Word of the Boston Tea Party spread, and other colonies threw their own tea parties.

About a month later, Britain retaliated with five punitive measures in the Coercive Acts of 1774, which, for example, ordered the port of Boston be closed to shipping until the colonies paid for the damages resulting from the Boston Tea Party. Unwilling to comply with the measures, the colonists labeled them the "Intolerable Acts," and began the process that eventually led them to declare their independence on July 4, 1776. Great Britain, however, ignored the Declaration of Independence and sent even more soldiers. Thus began the American Revolution (1776–1783).

At that point, Britain seized what it deemed an excellent opportunity to win the war: an offer of freedom to Africans in the colonies if they would fight for the mother country. About 25,000 enslaved African males accepted the offer.

Not to be outdone, the colonies—with the exception of Georgia and South Carolina—made a counter offer. At first, George Washington (1732–1799) vacillated over allowing Negroes to enlist in the Continental Army. He accepted them initially, then changed his mind, then allowed them to join when he knew he needed their help to win the war. Ultimately, at least 5,000 Negroes fought in the American Revolution.[4] While some were simply commended for their bravery, others were freed for heroic acts:

- Serving as a spy, James Amistead went from American camps to British camps, giving accurate information to the Americans and false to the British.[5]

- George Latchom fought alongside Colonel John Cropper. During a battle in Virginia, he killed a British soldier; later, he saved the colonel's life by pulling him from a waist-deep puddle of mud. Cropper purchased Latchom and set him free.[6]

- In exchange for his freedom, Austin Dabney took his master's place and became an artilleryman in the Georgia corps. The Georgia legislature awarded him 112 acres for his "bravery and fortitude."[7]

The immigrants' fight for freedom ended when Great Britain recognized the colonies' independence on September 3, 1783. Most of the Negro soldiers who fought for Britain were then transported to British colonies in the Caribbean, a few to Nova Scotia, and the remainder to England.

During the next four years, men known as the Founding Fathers wrote laws to govern their new republic. Unfortunately, the laws were drafted and adopted with the implicit understanding that they applied to white men only, as indicated in Article I, Section 2 of the Constitution, which specifies how a state's population is counted for representation, meaning to determine the number of representatives it will have in the House of Representatives:

- Free persons, including indentured servants, were counted.

- Native Americans ("Indians") who did not pay taxes were excluded.

- Each enslaved African was counted as three-fifths of a person.

   Note: The phrase "persons held to service or labor," not slave or African, is used in the Constitution. Women were counted, but they were not allowed to vote until 1920.

In 1788, the thirteen colonies became the United States of America with the ratification of the Constitution. However, old prejudices ran deep: the English scorned the Irish, who in turn shunned the Germans, who spurned newcomers from Italy, Poland, Russia, and other areas in southern and eastern Europe. Congress passed laws barring all Asians from entering the country.[8] Protestants denounced Catholics and some members of both denominations slighted Jewish immigrants. As a whole, the new nation kept Africans and Native Americans at a distance—the former enslaved, the latter on reservations.

After Vermont established the first Indian Reservation in 1786, other states followed suit. And the election of President Andrew Jackson (1787–1845) in 1828, followed by the Indian Removal Act of 1830, sealed the fate of Native Americans. Authorized to "negotiate removal treaties" with Native American nations east of the Mississippi River, Jackson offered them relocation expense and unsettled land in "Indian Territory," known as Oklahoma today, in exchange for their homelands. (Congress allotted $500,000 for transportation costs.) To coerce the nations to sign new treaties, Jackson told them the United States could not enforce its current ones, meaning it would not intervene when states, specifically Alabama, Georgia, and Mississippi, in violation of federal law and tribal regulations, placed the nations under state law.[9]

Initially, the act targeted the "Five Civilized Tribes"—Creek, Choctaw, Chickasaw, Cherokee, and Seminole—who were so labeled because they had adopted American customs such as plantation-style farming with slave labor, building their own schools, and publishing an "Indian" newspaper. But Jackson was determined to move all Native Americans to land west of the Mississippi.[10] Eventually, other nations were included with about 50,000 people relocating at an approximate cost of 40 to 60 million dollars.

Four notes here:

- The discovery of gold in Georgia in 1828 and the lucrative production of cotton in Alabama and Mississippi led white settlers and speculators to lobby for Native Americans' land in the Southeast.

- Without the protection of federal law and barred from testifying against whites by state law, warfare and the Supreme Court were Native Americans' only recourse against jealous whites who harassed them, stole their produce and livestock, and settled on their land.

- Each nation fought to remain in its homeland, but none longer than the Cherokee and the Seminole, the latter in three series of Seminole Wars until it had too few members to continue (1816–1819, 1835–1842, and 1855–1858), the former until it had exhausted all legal means and was forcibly removed by the military in 1838, along a route that became known as the "Trail of Tears," so named for the Cherokee's pain and suffering while traveling by foot, wagons, and horseback.[11] Over 4,000 died, some from diseases such as dysentery, cholera, and smallpox; others perished from preventable causes, which some consider genocide, for example: inadequate food, improper clothing, exposure to contagious diseases and the elements, lack of or improper medical care, and exhaustion, to name a few.

- Native Americans left over 15 million acres of land for white settlers in the Southeast. Most Native Americans living west of the Mississippi lost their lives and land to the discovery of gold in Colorado and California, and to the belief in "manifest destiny": a notion that the United States had a predetermined right to occupy all of North America.

While Native Americans were being placed on reservations, relocated, and massacred, abolitionists were breaking the chains of slavery, one state at a time. In 1777, Vermont abolished slavery, followed by Pennsylvania in 1780, and Massachusetts in 1783. But it wasn't until 1808 that the United States banned international slave trading.

The South, however, saw slavery differently.

To free their slaves meant giving up their way of life and having to contend with what was known in the North as a freedmen's problem.

Freedmen were not welcome in white society, hence the double-edged sword of being "free." Many whites feared that skilled colored men—particularly blacksmiths, carpenters, mechanics, jockeys, and groomsmen—might take jobs from white men. Simply stated, the problem was a question: How could the freedmen's unalienable right to life, liberty, and the pursuit of happiness be secured in a hostile environment?

Some saw sending them to Africa as the answer.

Believing Negroes would have a better life as free men in Africa than in America, Reverend Robert Finley (1772–1817) founded the American Colonization Society (ACS) for the sole purpose of transporting freedmen to a colony the organization planned to establish in Africa. To represent the freedmen's "liberated" status, the colony would be named Liberia.[12] With Bushrod Washington (1762–1829), the nephew of George Washington, as its president, the organization was supported by slaveholders, politicians, religious groups, and prominent citizens, such as Representative Daniel Webster (1772–1851); Francis Scott Key (1779–1843), composer of "The Star-Spangled Banner"; and Henry Clay (1777–1852), author of the Compromise of 1850. By 1835, the ACS had established six colonies on the West Coast of Africa. Between 1820 and 1830, about 1,000 freedmen settled in Liberia.[13] By one report, the majority of those who emigrated were ex-slaves whose manumission was granted on the condition that they move to Africa.[14]

Although some Negroes, led by shipping merchant Paul Cuffe (1759–1817), supported colonization, colored people were not allowed to become members of the ACS. Cuffe, possibly the wealthiest colored man in the United States at the time, had indeed transported 38 Negroes to Sierra Leone in 1815—two years before the ACS was formally organized. However, when a vote on colonization was taken at Bethel African Methodist Episcopal Church in Philadelphia on January 15, 1817, the 3,000 Negro men present unanimously voted nay.[15]

While the colonization effort stalled, the abolitionist movement accelerated, magnifying not only the freedmen's problem but also the nation's. Because products and property from slave states grew and sustained the economy nationwide, abolishing slavery threatened the United States's financial foothold. Cotton, the major export, was produced by slave labor, which was supplied by the interstate slave trade, which in turn grew the ship-building industry in Rhode Island. Mississippi produced the best grade of cotton, which kept the textile mills spinning in the Northeast. Slaves were used as collateral to secure loans to purchase land and additional slaves. All levels of government were supported by the taxes paid on those transactions.

With cotton and slaves as the country's most profitable commodities, an imbalance of free and slave states could jeopardize the nation's economy. Congress sought to eliminate the risk with compromises. First, the Missouri Compromise, passed in 1820, admitted one slave state and one free state: Missouri and Maine, respectively. Thirty years later, the infamous Compromise of 1850 included:

- admission of California as a free state

- banning the slave trade in Washington, D.C., but not slavery

- authorizing a $10 million payment to Texas to settle its boundary dispute with New Mexico

- placing no restriction on slavery in Utah and New Mexico territories
- passage of the Fugitive Slave Act, which mandated that runaways be returned to their owners and stripped Congress of any power over the slave trade among slaveholding states. (A note here: to replace the banned international slave trade, some southern slaveholders forced slaves to copulate with multiple partners, a practice known as breeding.)

While these and other compromises were made to sustain the economy, slaves waged their fights for freedom by secretly destroying crops, feigning illness, and attempting to or committing unthinkable acts, like those in the following stories:

A house slave named Celia (c.1836–1855), purchased by wealthy Missouri slaveholder Robert Newsom in 1850, was carrying his third child by her eighteenth birthday. Hoping to appease her friend George, also "owned" by Newsom, who had told her to refuse Newsom's advances, Celia warned him not to come to her cabin again. But after his adult daughters retired for the evening, Newsom crept to her shack anyway, leaving Celia no choice but to defend herself with a large stick. The next morning, Newsom's daughters discovered he was missing and sent for the sheriff. Through multiple interrogations, Celia maintained she knew nothing about Newsom's whereabouts. Eventually, however, she confessed: "As soon as I struck him the Devil got into me, and I struck him with the stick until he was dead, and then rolled him in the fire and burnt him up."[16]

Celia maintained that no one helped her. More than likely, the pent-up rage from five years of sexual assaults gave Celia the strength to avenge herself alone. Although Missouri law stated it was a crime for a man to "take any woman unlawfully against her will and by force, menace or duress, compelling her to be defiled," the judge did not allow Celia's attorney to instruct the jury that a slaveholder had no right to rape a slave and that Newsom's death could be considered justifiable homicide. If so instructed, the jury might have spared her life. Celia was executed on December 21, 1855.

A freedom fighter whose life was spared as an infant, Nat Turner (1800–1831) endured abandonment by his father—who fled for freedom when Nat was ten—the indignity of seeking permission and a pass to visit his wife Cherry and their son Reddick who lived on another plantation, at least one brutal beating for advocating abolition, and adapting to four "masters." By the age of twenty-three, he was owned by his fourth master, ten-year-old Putnam Moore, stepson of wealthy plantation owner Joseph Travis. Turner was one of seventeen slaves who worked Travis's 400 acres.[17]

After learning to read, possibly from his ten-year-old owner, and studying the Bible, Turner grew to despise slavery like his African-born mother Nancy did. Distraught over giving birth to a slave, Nancy would have killed her newborn had she not been restrained.

Turner's knowledge of the Bible earned him the

respect of both slaveholders and slaves: the former used the Bible to justify slavery; the Africans saw it as a denouncement of the injustice of slavery. After Turner became a minister, Travis hired him out to preach to slaves on adjacent plantations. From the choice Turner made, one can deduce that Travis either kept the earnings or gave Turner such a small amount that he chose to follow what he believed was his God-given purpose—to liberate the slaves—rather than save to purchase his own freedom.

Considered a mystic by some and blessed by God by his family (based on birthmarks), Turner saw the solar eclipse in February 1831 as a sign to begin his mission. Thus he started recruiting.

On the night of August 22, 1831, Turner and six recruits—Hark Moore, Henry Porter, Nelson Edwards, Sam Francis, Will Francis, and Jack Reese—began their fight for freedom. By the next morning, another nine men had joined the group. Within two days the recruits had grown to seventy and about fifty-five whites had been killed, women and children included. However, with increasing armed resistance from local whites, the arrival of the state militia, and the loss of recruits' lives, Turner's group was forced to disperse on the third day. Within a few hours all the men—except for Turner—were caught and immediately executed. For revenge, irate whites burned, maimed, and tortured innocent Negroes. After evading authorities for nine weeks, Turner was captured and brought to trial. Although he pled not guilty, Turner was convicted of murder and hanged.

In 1830, the population of Southampton, Virginia,

consisted of 6,573 whites, 1,745 free blacks, and 7,756 enslaved Africans.[18] Can you imagine what might have happened if Turner's plan to kill whites, take their weapons, and arm the slaves had worked?

But Turner's were not the only extreme measures . . .

John Brown (1800–1859), a conductor on the Underground Railroad, grew up in Connecticut with religious parents who adamantly opposed slavery. After living in Pennsylvania, Massachusetts, New York, and Ohio, Brown moved to Osawatomie, Kansas. I suspect he, like many others, migrated west to take advantage of cheap land and thereby improve his lot. From his actions, it seems Brown was also determined to keep the Kansas Territory free of slavery. He is said to have massacred five men. His assault was one of several clashes between abolitionists and pro-slavers. All told, skirmishes between the groups resulted in over 200 injuries and fatalities, giving the area the moniker "Bleeding Kansas." Blood, however, was not shed in Kansas alone.

Massachusetts' Senator Charles Sumner (1811–1874) was a constitutional scholar, resolute abolitionist, and an erudite but long-winded speaker: he took over three hours to declare the Fugitive Slave Act and the entire Compromise of 1850 as violations of the Constitution. But, beginning on May 19, 1856, he spent two days—speaking five hours each day—denouncing the Kansas-Nebraska Act in his speech "The Crime Against Kansas," during which—among other unflattering remarks—he said of Senator Andrew Butler (1796–1857):

> The senator from South Carolina has read many books of chivalry, and believes himself a chivalrous knight with sentiments of honor and courage. Of course, he has chosen a mistress to whom he has made vows, and who, though ugly to others, is always lovely to him; though polluted in the sight of the world, is chaste in his sight, I mean the harlot, slavery.[4]

Though well-spoken, those were fighting words! Senator Butler's nephew, Representative Preston Brooks (1819–1857), fumed for two days before avenging his uncle. On May 22, 1856, while Sumner sat at his desk in the Senate Chamber, Brooks attacked him and repeatedly struck his head with a cane.[20]

The House of Representatives lacked the votes to expel Brooks, but a Baltimore court fined him $300. After he resigned, in protest of the attempt to expel him and as a ploy for a special election, South Carolinians re-elected him to a full term. Sworn into office August 1, 1856, Brooks died only five months later at the age of thirty-seven on January 2, 1857.

Senator Sumner, who had been beaten unconscious, spent three and a half years as an invalid. Left with life-long headaches, he returned to the senate and served an additional fourteen years, during which he introduced a civil rights bill to mandate equal accommodations in all public places. Sumner died of a heart attack in his home at the age of seventy-three.

By the way, Senator Sumner declared the Compromise of 1850 unconstitutional because the word "slave" is not even in the Constitution. As previously noted, the Founding Fathers used the phrase "person held to service or labour" as a synonym for slave. The word slavery did not appear in the Constitution until the passage of the Thirteenth Amendment in 1865.

As for Kansas and John Brown, Kansas entered the Union as a free state in 1861. John Brown waged his fight for freedom in Kansas and Missouri for two years before returning to the east to do the same. On October 16, 1859, he and twenty-one men broke into the federal armory at Harpers Ferry, Virginia, planning to take its weapons, establish an army, kill all the white people (in slaveholding states), and thereby abolish slavery. Bad weather, a shortage of men, and tactical miscalculations prevented them from doing so.

Brown's failed mission did little to alleviate the whites' fear of more uprisings. And similar to the aftermath of Nat Turner's fight for freedom, pro-slavery bullies beat and harassed anyone they suspected to be anti-slavery. Their fear might have been justified if the slaves and freedmen shown in the 1850 census had joined forces, armed themselves, and declared war on slaveholders.

1850 UNITED STATES FEDERAL CENSUS

| State | Whites | Free Colored | Slaves |
|---|---|---|---|
| Virginia | 894,149 | 53,906 | 473,026 |
| North Carolina | 552,477 | 27,271 | 218,412 |
| Georgia | 513,083 | 2,586 | 362,966 |
| Alabama | 426,515 | 2,250 | 342,894 |
| Mississippi | 291,536 | 898 | 300,419 |
| South Carolina | 274,775 | 8,769 | 384,925 |
| Louisiana | 254,271 | 15,685 | 230,807 |

Of note here is that contrary to the widespread slave ownership these numbers appear to suggest, only about a third of white southerners were slave owners at that time. Small farmers with one to twenty slaves comprised 23 percent of the slaveholding population; mega slave owners made up about one percent. For example, eleven families owned 500 or more slaves, 254 owned 200 or more, and 8,000 owned 50 or more.[21]

BY THE MID-1800s, the United States was deadlocked over the issue of slavery. Congressmen debated and compromised; abolitionists called for an immediate end to slavery; pro-slavers, particularly those in the South, opposed any intervention by the federal government. It would take the election of a biased, but brilliant, president who loved his country enough to do what was necessary to keep it united before the question of slavery would be resolved.

Although he did not win the popular vote, Abraham Lincoln was elected president with a majority of the electoral votes—180 of 303. His opponents J.C. Breckenridge, Stephen A. Douglas, and John Bell received 72, 12, and 39 respectively.

In his inaugural address, Lincoln said, "I have no purpose, directly or indirectly, to interfere with the institution of slavery in the states where it exists. I believe I have no lawful right to do so, and I have no inclination to do so."[22]

Responding to journalist Horace Greeley's request that he use executive power and free the slaves, Lincoln declared:

. . . If there be those who would not save the Union unless they could at the same time destroy slavery, I do not agree with them. My paramount object is to save the Union and not either to save or destroy slavery.[23]

For his candor, Lincoln was known as Honest Abe, but it appears southerners had concerns about his honesty before his March 4 inaugural address. By February 4, 1861, South Carolina, Mississippi, Florida, Georgia, Alabama, and Texas had seceded from the Union and started the process of forming a constitution and electing their own president, Jefferson Davis. Upon the completion of that process, which formalized their secession from the United States (the Union), those states became the Confederate States of America, a separate entity not subject to or protected by the laws of the United States of America.

The Confederacy demanded the surrender of all Union forts in the South, but President Lincoln refused to do so. Consequently, on April 21, 1861, Confederate troops attacked Fort Sumter in Charleston, South Carolina. Thus began the four-year American Civil War. Soon thereafter, Arkansas, Virginia, North Carolina, and Tennessee seceded from the Union. Without the intervention of federal authorities, "the border states"—Delaware, Kentucky, Maryland, and Missouri—probably would have done so too.

With twice as many states, the Union appeared to have an advantage, but during the first two years, Confederate soldiers won more battles than the Union Army—perhaps because southern troops were fighting on their own turf, or perhaps before becoming soldiers, some of the young men had ridden horses and hunted for sport. Consequently, they were more skilled marksmen than their northern counterparts, many of whom were poor city boys, lacking not only in horsemanship and marksmanship but also in familiarity with the terrain. What's more, Union troops were traveling longer distances, adjusting to a new climate, and becoming familiar with the area—all while trying to kill in order not to be killed. And when they did win a battle, unlike the Southern troops, they had to find a safe place to guard and hold their Confederate captives. I imagine those young men cried, "Help!"

Perhaps their cry was heard on the night of May 23, 1861: Africans Frank Baker, Sheppard Mallory, and James Townsend escaped from a Confederate unit and sought asylum at Fort Monroe, Virginia, a Union fort. The men were building fortifications for the 115th Virginia Militia, a Confederate unit. After overhearing their owner discuss his plans to send them to North Carolina to do the same job, the men fled. Under the moonlight, they rowed a Confederate boat across the harbor to Fort Monroe.

The next morning, Major General Benjamin Franklin Butler (1818–1893), the fort's commanding officer, interviewed the fugitives. Although impressed by the military intelligence they provided, he dallied over granting the men asylum. While he was weighing his options, a confederate officer arrived at the fort to claim the Africans, per the Fugitive Slave Law. However,

Virginia had seceded from the Union on April 17, 1861. Butler, a practicing attorney before joining the Army, reminded the officer that Virginia's succession rendered it a foreign country, which meant it was neither protected nor bound by United States laws. Then, shooing the officer away, he declared his right by military law to keep "enemy property" that was being used against the Union. Thus Baker, Mallory, and Townsend were given asylum as contraband (confiscated enemy property).

Within four months, Congress passed the Confiscation Act of 1861 authorizing the seizure, confiscation, and condemnation of "any property of whatever kind," including "any person claimed to be held to labor or service (a slave)," that was being used against the United States. A year later, the Confiscation Act of 1862 expanded the seizure to include all property whether being used against the Union or not. Both Confiscation Acts, which President Lincoln opposed in fear of the four border states seceding as well, "freed" Africans in the Confederate States first as "property" owned by the military, then as that of civilians. It's interesting here to note that Lincoln persuaded Congress to pass a resolution that would have compensated the border states had they initiated a plan of gradual emancipation, but the states refused the offer.

This leads me to the mythical Emancipation Proclamation, which literally freed no one.

When free Negroes volunteered to join the Union Army, Lincoln initially declined their offer, allegedly believing that accepting Negroes would alienate Northern whites and jeopardize support of the border states. But, in an act designed to preserve the union, Lincoln issued the Emancipation Proclamation on January 1, 1863, in which he stated "all persons held as slaves in any state in rebellion against the United States are and henceforward shall be free."[24]

What's crucial to point out here is that in the document, Lincoln specifically named the ten Confederate states. But those states—having seceded from the United States, established their own constitution, and elected a president (Jefferson Davis, 1808–1889)—were not bound by his executive order. Furthermore, the four slave-holding border states had rejected Lincoln's offer of reimbursement for gradually freeing enslaved Africans. Thus, the Emancipation Proclamation did not free a single slave. Yet the myth lives on. Issuing the Emancipation Proclamation was merely a military strategy Lincoln used to secure the manpower and local know-how he needed to win the war. Hence, the moniker given to him of The Great Emancipator is a misnomer. Admittedly, in his letter to Horace Greeley, he indicated he saw it his duty as president to abide by the Constitution, which meant leaving slavery intact, but that personally, he would have preferred freedom for everyone.

Although about 100,000 African men joined the Army after the Emancipation Proclamation, Negroes had begun joining Union units in May 1861, over a year and a half before the document was signed. It seems the Africans' rapid word-of-mouth communication network translated the asylum granted to Baker, Mallory, and Townsend to mean slaves could emancipate themselves by fleeing to Union forts or joining Union lines—and they did both. By Sunday, May 26, 1861, eight more Africans came to Fort Monroe, and by Monday an additional forty-seven had arrived. By the end of June, the fort had over 500 Negroes, and by the end of the war over 10,000.[25]

Union forts throughout the South were overrun by fleeing African families. When they could not be accommodated inside the forts, the Africans built structures outside and earned their keep by cleaning, cooking, laundering, and digging latrines. The sites they built became known as "contraband camps," with growing populations throughout the war. One camp in Mississippi, called the Corinth Contraband Camp, grew to approximately 6,000 between April 1862 until December 1863, at which time the freed Africans were moved to President's Island Contraband Camp in Memphis, Tennessee. Not much remains of the homes, hospital, and school built at the camp. However, the site is now a historic park with the eponymous name "Corinth Contraband Camp."

Overall, an estimated 179,000 African men served in the Army during the Civil War, and 19,000 served in the Navy. Prejudice relegated most of the men to positions such as carpenters, chaplains, cooks, guards, spies, steamboat pilots, and surgeons, but there were also many Africans—including Robert Smalls, Mary Bowser, and Harriett Tubman—who provided intelligence to Union troops.

> Robert Smalls, an enslaved African in South Carolina, worked on the *CSS*, a cotton steamer the Confederate Army had converted into a gunboat. After the white captain and his crew went ashore, Smalls smuggled his family and a few friends aboard and set sail. To avoid other Confederate vessels scattered throughout the area, Smalls had memorized their positions, the signals necessary for safe passage, and the route to Union ships. Entering the route, he raised a white flag and surrendered the vessel to the United States Navy.

> Mary Bowser (1839?–?) was freed and educated at the Quaker School for Negroes in Philadelphia, courtesy of Elizabeth Van Lew, her former owner. Van Lew

arranged for Bowser to work as a servant for Jefferson Davis. "Wearing the mask" while performing her duties from 1863 to 1864, Bowser feigned dim-wittedness and used her photographic memory to gather and report Confederate strategies to Van Lew, who passed the information on to her contacts in the Union Army. Realizing that she herself was being spied upon, Bowser attempted to burn Davis's home before she successfully escaped.[26]

⚮

Harriet Tubman—chief of the most successful covert operation in the country, the Underground Railroad—left that post to serve as cook, nurse, and intelligence agent for the Union Army.

According to "How Slavery Really Ended in America," an article in *The New York Times Magazine* on March 4, 2011, colored men were the best source of information for Lincoln's master intelligence agent, Allan Pinkerton. With the addition of African manpower and local intelligence, our country's second fight for freedom ended on April 9, 1865, when General Robert E. Lee surrendered to General Ulysses S. Grant at Appomattox Court House, Virginia. Located near Lynchburg, the town is now a national historic park.

AFTER THE CIVIL WAR, Negroes were homeless, desperate, and unemployed. Some lived off the land and escaped the elements in whatever shelter they could find. Thousands made their homes at contraband camps, some of which were so shoddy and squalid that at least 25 percent of the refugees lost their lives to either crime, disease, or exposure.[27]

To alleviate the Negroes' suffering, the federal government established the Freedmen Bureau on March 3, 1865. Officially known as the Bureau of Refugees, Freedmen and Abandoned Lands, the bureau was authorized to provide a variety of services, including providing food, clothing, and shelter for destitute and suffering refugees and freedmen, and to reserve up to forty acres of abandoned land in the Confederacy for every male citizen, whether refugee or freedman.[28]

The Bureau operated without bias: impoverished whites, who also suffered terribly during and after the war, received about six million of almost 21 million rations issued during the bureau's first four years. The Bureau also founded or provided financial aid to most of the colleges now known as Historically Black Colleges and Universities (HBCU). Charitable contributions enabled the Bureau to continue its educational programs until 1872, eight years longer than it was authorized to operate.

As for the forty acres, General William Tecumseh Sherman (1820–1891) issued Special Field Order 15, which gave each Negro settler "possessory title" to forty-acre plots of coastal land in South Carolina, Georgia, and Florida. In addition, some were given mules Union troops no longer needed. However, President Andrew Johnson (1808–1875) revoked the order and mandated the land be returned to the former owners. Neither the elocution of Senator Charles Sumner nor the fervor of Representative Thaddeus Stevens could garner enough votes for Congress to pass legislation that would have allowed Negroes to keep the land or to receive compensation for their slave labor. Nonetheless, Sumner and Stevens never wavered in their efforts to make equality a reality for former slaves.

Sumner submitted a Civil Rights bill that would have

banned racial discrimination and segregation in education, all public places and transportation, and even in churches and cemeteries. Stevens, an Underground Railroad agent before becoming a congressman, joined Sumner in drafting the conditions under which the South would be brought back into the Union, the most significant being prohibiting slavery, making a loyalty oath to the US, and rewriting their state constitutions.

Although rejoining the Union was the best option for the South to rebuild its economy, the conditions were not accepted unanimously. Consequently, to ensure each state complied with the provisions, Union troops remained in the South for several years during Reconstruction, the twelve-year process of bringing the South back into the Union as free states.

During that time, Congress began writing belated "thank-you notes" to Negroes in the form of the Thirteenth, Fourteenth, and Fifteenth Amendments to the Constitution. The notes abolished slavery in 1865, acknowledged Negroes as citizens in 1868, and gave them the right to vote in 1879. Subsequently, Negroes were elected and served at the local, state, and national levels of government in South Carolina, Mississippi, Louisiana, Florida, North Carolina, Alabama, Georgia, and Virginia.

Although ten of the twenty-two who served in Congress had attended college, and five were attorneys, many of their white colleagues were suspect, creating dissension with accusations of corruption. I should note here that some of those elected were freedmen who had been educated in freedmen schools staffed by northern whites, and some had even attended schools in the North. Becoming educated was not a crime for freedmen, and a few of those who learned taught others, sometimes at what was called "Sunday school."

But I digress . . .

BY THE 1890s, Negroes had lost their political punch and would not be elected to national offices again until 1928.

Having ousted Negro politicians—and leaning on Jim Crow laws and Black Codes that were based on a belief that Negroes must be kept in their place, separate from and subservient to whites—white legislators restored some of the South's "traditions." This meant that Negroes and whites could not use the same public facilities such as pools, water fountains, restrooms, and waiting rooms. Owners of hotels and restaurants, and even ministers, closed their doors to colored people. So did the justice system, prohibiting Negroes from serving on juries or appearing as witnesses, as well as allowing unemployed Negroes to be tried for vagrancy and auctioned off to white employers who paid their fines. In some states, Negroes could not be out after dark or walk on the same sidewalk as whites.

To prevent Negroes from exercising their voting rights, Southern legislatures passed strict voter-registration laws, one of which required passing a literacy test. Although some Negro men could read, they couldn't read well enough to pass literacy tests, which were often rigged. But regardless of tests and the ever-present challenge to comply with Jim Crow laws, some Negro men exercised their rights; others chose not to jeopardize their lives or subject their families to white supremacists' terrorist attacks by attempting to do so. But it seems they all agreed on one thing: if Negroes did not become literate while adapting to freedom, their rights and privileges as citizens would be compromised at best or never fully realized at worst. In like manner, more education for whites would facilitate their adapting to a livelihood free of slavery as well.

With at least 90 percent of its Negro population illiterate, the South attempted to reduce that percentage by establishing public schools. In writing new constitutions—one of the conditions required for readmission to the Union—each former Confederate state adopted a constitution requiring the establishment of public schools for all students, regardless of race, class, or financial status. In fact, Louisiana's new constitution specifically restricted the state from establishing separate schools for any race, while Mississippi's and South Carolina's specified integrated schools.[29]

Philanthropic organizations from the North sent colored and white teachers to the South to teach Negroes of all ages—in schools at contraband camps, in those built by the Freedmen's Bureau, in churches, and most importantly, in schools built by Negroes themselves. During the decade 1867 to 1877, southern whites and Negroes freely mingled, and their children attended the same public schools.[30] But when politics entered the picture, whites demanded separate schools.

Committed to education and lacking funds to build and maintain enough schools for their communities, Negroes were obliged to accept segregated public schools. Consequently, Negro students attended inferior schools that had ill-equipped labs, an ongoing shortage of supplies, and old textbooks, which were transferred from white schools, with often missing or defamed pages.

Oral African American history indicates that the Constitution was not in books supplied to Negro schools, a purposeful omission designed to keep the Negro in his place by keeping him ignorant of his rights. Like in Swan Lake, most rural areas in the South had no public schools for colored people before the early 1900s.

Negroes who preferred to provide their own education and govern themselves did so by combining their resources and acquiring land to build their own all-black towns. Sixty such municipalities were founded between 1865 and 1915, providing their residents a lifestyle comparable to, and in some cases superior to, neighboring white towns.

A prime example, Mound Bayou, Mississippi, is thought to be the first of these towns. Two cousins, Isaiah T. Montgomery and Benjamin Green, founded Mound Bayou in 1887, with the goal of making it a haven for Negroes who valued education, economic growth, and self-sufficiency. Populated by doctors, farmers, lawyers, entrepreneurs, and teachers, the town grew to 8,000 by 1911. Because crime was virtually nonexistent, the people are said to have demolished the jail.

Leon and Aura Kruger moved from Boston, Massachusetts, to Mound Bayou in 1967, becoming the town's second white family. Advocates for civil and human rights, Leon established a much-needed medical clinic, while Aura taught at the high school. Their daughter, Jo, only ten when her family moved, recounts her family's Mound Bayou experience in *The Outskirts of Hope*, penned under her married name of Jo Ivester.

In its heyday, Mound Bayou had public and private schools, forty businesses, six churches, three cotton gins, a bank, a sawmill, a library, a swimming pool, a hospital, and its own newspaper. When the price of cotton fell, so did production, along with Mound Bayou's economy and its population. Like other small towns and rural areas in the South, colored people left Mound Bayou for better opportunities, especially in education, their weapon of choice in the fight for civil rights. Today, Mound Bayou's population of 1,517 is 98.6 percent African American.

In a manner similar to Mound Bayou's founders, wealthy Negro O.W. Gurley, who owned land in Arkansas, purchased 40 acres in Oklahoma with the designation that they be sold only to colored people. From all indications, the purchasers made Gurley proud. The property they bought in 1906 and named Greenwood grew in such affluence that it came to be known nationwide by the moniker "Negro Wall Street." It seems the well-run businesses—including hotels, law and doctors' offices, cafés, nightclubs, pharmacies, and grocery stores—as well as churches and beautifully constructed homes were beyond compare, but irksome to envious whites who destroyed the area in 1921.

Rumors of a colored man's arrest for allegedly molesting a white elevator operator led to a riot when a group of Negro men went to the jail to spirit him away safely. Racist whites looted the black-owned businesses, set fires to commercial and residential properties, and injured scores of residents. Over 300 people were killed, and more than 900 were left homeless. Despite the losses, within five years, Negroes rebuilt their community, which is known today as the Greenwood Historic District in Tulsa, Oklahoma.

Allensworth, California, a once flourishing black town, is also a historic site. Established in 1908, the town was named to honor one of its founders, Allen Allensworth (1842–1914), an escaped African who became the first black lieutenant colonel in the Union Army. Located in Tulare county, Allensworth boasted a school, public library, hotel, and church. Tragically, Col. Allensworth succumbed to injuries sustained when he was struck by a motorcyclist.

Without its leader, the once thriving Allensworth struggled to remain afloat. Unfortunately, a steadily decreasing population—the result of young people migrating to urban areas—and the discovery of arsenic in its water supply in 1966 led to the town's closing. On October 6, 1976, the area was dedicated as Colonel Allensworth State Historic Park.

## ♫ *Accompaniments* ♫

℗

*While I have attempted to briefly recap our country's early history, Neil Diamond's "America" tells the immigrants' stories better than I ever could. Thanks to the flights and fights of real patriots, heroes, and heroines in past eras, I have "The House I Live In." Kudos to Frank Sinatra and Neil Diamond for describing "What Is America to Me?" And also to Lamin as he comes to know the "American Anthem" as intimately as Nora Jones sings it.*

*It must have been a "Great Day" when enslaved Africans emancipated themselves. How they may have sung "Slavery Chain Done Broke at Last" as they made their way to contraband camps.*

*About the name Jim Crow: historians differ on the origin of the phrase. By one report, James (Jim) was a slave who took his owner's last name Crow. A crippled stableman, Jim sang and danced while he worked. As I've mentioned previously, enslaved Africans often communicated with each other in codes and double-talk such as these lyrics, which appear to mock ever-watchful overseers or slaveholders who addressed all Africans as girls or boys.*

> *Come listen all you galls and boys,*
> *I'm going to sing a little song,*
> *My name is Jim Crow.*
> *Weel about and turnabout and do jis so,*
> *Eb'ry time I weel about I jump Jim Crow.*

*It is speculated that the white actor Thomas Rice saw Jim singing and dancing and wrote the music for the song. To* mimic Jim, Rice performed in blackface, makeup that white actors used to darken their faces so they could portray vile stereotypes of Negroes.31 While as a grotesquely stereotypical Negro, he undoubtedly was entertaining to his audience whom the song was ridiculing. But, like Rice, they didn't get it because "crow" was one of the unflattering words whites used for colored people.

Eventually, the phrase came to represent the discriminatory practices that kept Negroes separate from and subservient to whites.

# Stony the
# Road

The lack of schools for Negroes in Swan Lake was one of the most injurious lingering effects of slavery. But Swan Lake was not alone. Throughout the South, in rural communities that had schools, Negro students were instructed in small churches, abandoned cabins, or poorly constructed buildings that barely sheltered them from the elements; and their instructors had only a grade-school education. Thanks to the vision shared by a group of Negroes in Tuskegee, Alabama, educator Booker T. Washington (1856–1915), and philanthropist Julius Rosenwald (1862–1932), this situation began to change in 1912.

To ensure that students in their area would be taught by trained teachers, leaders of the Tuskegee Negro Community approached the Alabama legislature for funds to start a normal school. Around 1880, the legislature allotted an annual $2,000 stipend for instructors' salaries. With their goal achieved, the leaders then hired Washington as the first teacher at Tuskegee Normal School for Youth, which existed only on paper when he arrived in Alabama in June 1881.[1]

A natural-born salesman with impeccable manners, Washington, the son of an enslaved African housekeeper and an unknown white man, quickly made friends while looking for a building to use as a school. A run-down shack near an African Methodist Episcopal church was the only suitable place he could find; however, the leaky roof forced Washington to search for better accommodations. In a few months, he found for sale a former plantation with an old mansion, which he visualized as his new schoolhouse. Reluctantly, he borrowed $250 from a friend to pay half the asking price for the property.

With local colored people contributing building materials and technical expertise, residents throughout the county donating money, and students providing labor, Washington began the process of transforming the plantation into Tuskegee Institute. (The students' ages ranged from fifteen to the late-thirties.)[2]

To ensure Tuskegee's financial security and attract students who met his criteria—having a grade-school education by trained teachers—Washington went on a mission to establish an endowment for the institute and to build elementary schools for Negro students in adjacent communities. He accomplished his mission with moral and financial support from many individuals, but no one contributed more to the school-building project than Julius Rosenwald.

The son of middle-class German Jewish immigrants, Rosenwald rose from a humble position as a summer clerk and delivery boy for a $0.49–$0.99 store to president and CEO of Sears, Roebuck & Co.[3] It seems he and Washington validated their mutual admiration upon meeting for the first time, with Washington seeing him as a new board member. After a polite period of time had passed, he invited Rosenwald to serve on Tuskegee's Board. But Rosenwald declined at least twice, choosing to send boxes of shoes to Tuskegee's students instead. In his thank-you note, Washington emphasized that the students were not simply given the shoes, they were required to pay any affordable amount for each pair, with some paying as much as a dollar. Impressed, Rosenwald sent another batch; and by 1917, he had not only become a Tuskegee trustee, he had also established the Rosenwald Fund. With a goal of helping build 5,000 schools for colored students in rural areas in Alabama and fourteen additional southern states, he earmarked a portion of the fund for that purpose. (By one report, 639 schools were built in Mississippi, but none in Swan Lake).[4]

Initially, Rosenwald paid 50 percent of the construction costs and stipulated that Negroes match his contribution. Later, the matching was reduced to 25 percent from the Rosenwald Fund, 25 percent from African Americans, and 50 percent from other sources, including each state's board of education. Overall, Rosenwald contributed at least $4.3 million, and Negroes raised $4.7 million, which included land and labor. When Washington died in 1915, Tuskegee had an endowment of $2 million and seventy-five grade schools had been built. By the time of his passing in 1932, Rosenwald had helped build 5,300 state-of-the-art educational facilities that came to be known as Rosenwald Schools.[5]

None of the schools bore his name because he preferred they not be eponymous. However, they were easily identified by a common design, which featured banks of large windows for maximizing natural light; breeze windows for improving ventilation; and removable partitions for changing the size of a room or converting the building to a larger school, an auditorium, or a community center. In addition, the lots were not less than two acres; the landscaping included a garden and a playground, and the schools were placed in a direction for the best exposure to the sun for heat. Each school had cloakrooms and two outhouses—the latter provided by the board of education. Most importantly, the length of the school year was set so that students spent more time in the classroom than in bean, corn, or cotton fields.

Over half a million colored students received their education in Rosenwald Schools. But, enrollments at the schools dropped as Negroes left rural areas and small towns in the South for better opportunities in the North. Attendance steadily decreased as more southern states began to desegregate schools in the late 1950s through the 1960s. Gradually, the schools fell into disuse and eventually closed. Most of the remaining ones are in an almost unrecognizable state of disrepair; the few that have been restored are used for other purposes. Because the schools are among the most endangered places of historical significance, steps are being taken to identify and document them as Rosenwald Schools, which brings me to a few documented cases that Lamin may not have heard about during African American History Month.

Although Negroes were denied the privilege of applying for patents before 1868, colored scientists had received over 300 by the early 1900s.[6] Inventor Granville T. Woods (1856–1910) registered almost sixty, of which thirty-five were for electrical devices, including the following three that are among his most important:

- The telegraphony, introduced in 1885, allowed messages to be sent by voice and Morse code over a single line.

- Patented in 1887, the Synchronous Multiplex Railway Telegraph transmitted messages to and from moving trains, enabling engineers to alert each other of hazards on the track, their respective locations, and thereby avoid collisions, delays, and costly repairs.

- Patented in 1901, the 3rd Rail Power Distribution system was implemented on subway, railway, and rapid transit lines around the world. It is still used in the New York City Subway System.[7] Like the name suggests, the system employs a third rail for collecting and distributing electrical power—making tunnel construction and underground train operation more efficient.

Wood's inventions caught the eyes of telephone inventor Alexander Graham Bell (1847–1922) and light bulb inventor Thomas Edison (1847–1931). Bell purchased Woods's patent for the multiplex telegraph, but Edison sued, claiming he invented the device first. Woods wasn't deterred, though. He used the proceeds from selling his patent to invent more products, and possibly to win the case Edison filed against him. Not willing to accept defeat, Edison offered Woods an executive position with his own Edison Electric Light Company. But Woods, who was largely self-taught, declined the offer, devoted more time to research, and founded his own company.

The lubricator cup patented by Elijah McCoy (1844–1929) in 1872 was also impressive. Born in Canada to former slaves who returned to the United States after the Civil War, McCoy received training as an engineer in Scotland. Because black engineers were not employed by most American companies, he accepted a position of fireman and oiler for the Michigan Central

Railroad. Overqualified for both and said to have become bored with the latter, McCoy envisioned the
trains oiling themselves. Unable to shake the image, he
conducted experiments until his lubricator cup was
perfected. By automatically oiling a machine's moving
parts that required lubricating, the cup eliminated the
need to turn off equipment for manual oiling, like
McCoy had to do when trains were resting at the station. The device worked so well, customers requested
"only the real McCoy." (Today the phrase is used to
describe perfection, as in a flawless product or performance.) In all, McCoy received over fifty patents for
modifying and updating the lubricator cup.[8]

Credited with more than 100 patents, chemist Percy
Julian (1899–1975) was world renowned as a leader in
creating products by synthesis, the process of turning
one substance into another by a series of planned
chemical reactions. For one example, Julian used the
African calabar bean to synthesize a drug used to treat
glaucoma. Later, using the soybean—and then the yam
—he made a synthetic cortisone that reduced the cost
of treating rheumatoid arthritis from hundreds of dollars per drop to pennies per ounce. Further, from soybean oil he extracted sterols, which he used to synthesize the female and male hormones of progesterone and
testosterone. Today, progesterone is used in hormone
replacement therapy and to prevent uterine cancer.[9]

In the field of medicine, Dr. Daniel Hale Williams (1856–1931) secured the support of Negro ministers, physicians, and businessmen to found a hospital and nurse training school. Opened in Chicago, Illinois, as Provident Hospital in 1891, the facility was the nation's first hospital to extend staff privileges to Negro and white physicians and to admit patients regardless of race. It was also the first nursing school for Negroes, and, by some reports, the site of the nation's first successful open-heart surgery.

On July 10, 1893, while treating a stab wound to the chest, Dr. Williams opened the patient's thoracic cavity, examined the heart, and sutured a nick in the pericardium, the membranous sac around the heart. The patient lived another twenty years.

Known as "father of the blood bank," Dr. Charles Drew (1904–1950) is acknowledged worldwide for his firsts:

- The method for long-term storage of plasma—the clear, yellow liquid part of blood that remains after cells and platelets are removed

- America's first large-scale blood bank, the "bloodmobiles," blood-donation vehicles such as busses or vans that are fully equipped to draw and store blood. Initially, trucks with refrigerators were used.

- First African American director of the Red Cross

Despite worldwide recognition of Dr. Drew's research and expertise, the Red Cross initially excluded him and all Negroes from donating blood. After years of disregarding scientific proof that blood differs only by type, not by race, the Red Cross lifted the exclusion, but with the provision that blood donated by whites and Negroes be stored separately.

Dr. Drew did not "wear the mask." Instead, he challenged the organization's covert racism, openly calling its policy of segregating blood unscientific and insulting. How much more he might have contributed to science and humanity had he survived injuries from a car accident in Burlington, North Carolina, on April 1, 1950!

LIKE IN THE Red Cross, covert racism was prevalent in other businesses in the North. For example, colored carpenters, mechanics, and painters often applied for jobs unaware they would be rejected because prejudiced white northerners refused to work with them. Consequently, African Americans worked diligently at whatever jobs they could find. College graduates accepted employment as porters, elevator operators, maids, butlers, window washers, chauffeurs, custodians, bellmen, busboys, dishwashers, etc. Creative artists resorted to menial positions too, except for those who found work in the entertainment industry during the Harlem Renaissance.

Because many artists and activists who migrated to New York City congregated in the area known as Harlem, the period from the early 1900s through the late 1930s is usually called the Harlem Renaissance, but it is also known as the New Negro Renaissance—a time of flourishing creativity and widespread appreciation of African American artists. For the first time in our country's history, William Grant Still's *Afro-American Symphony* was played by major symphony orchestras. At theaters and other venues, whites saw colored literary artists read, recite, or perform their works; and New York's nightclubs and concert halls booked African American bands, dancers, and singers.

But while Negro dancers and musicians lit up the clubs in New York, Black Codes still ruled. Colored entertainers, who were booked to perform for whites-only audiences, could not dine or dance in the clubs, and they could not enter or leave through the front doors. Thus, many artists joined activists and intellectuals in demanding civic, economic, and social justice.

In the literary world, Zora Neale Hurston (1891–1960) and Langston Hughes (1902–1967) may have been the most outspoken.

Born in Alabama, Hurston grew up in Eatonville, Florida, a town founded by Negroes in 1887. An anthropologist, sociologist, and author, Hurston published the first book of Negro folklore, *Mules and Men.* Before being published, these beliefs, customs, riddles, tales, and traditions were passed down orally.

Hurston was unabashedly forthright. Although some harshly criticized her position on desegregating public schools, she maintained that the presence of whites had no effect on education if Negro students attended schools equipped with adequate supplies and staffed by trained colored instructors. Only after her death did she receive the recognition she deserved. Published in 1937, her novel *Their Eyes Were Watching God* is one of *TIME* Magazine's 100 Best English-Language Novels Since 1923, the year the magazine was first published.

Similarly, in poems, short stories, essays, biographies, and plays, Langston Hughes—possibly the most powerful and prolific literary voice during his time—embraced the Negroes' culture and echoed their cry for civil and economic liberation. A poet at an early age, Hughes was nineteen when his poem *The Negro Speaks of Rivers* was published in the NAACP's *Crisis*, the most influential Negro magazine at the time. Four years later, his *Weary Blues* won *Opportunity* magazine's First Prize for Poetry. Hughes authored ten books of poetry, six works of fiction, five books of humor, six works for young people, and one anthology. He also co-authored three history books.

In a class of his own, James Weldon Johnson (1871–1938) has been called an American Renaissance man. Learned in languages, music, literature, and jurisprudence, Johnson was the first Negro to pass the bar and practice law in Florida. He was also a teacher, novelist, poet, and an editor. He is perhaps best known for writing the poem that his brother Rosamond (1873–1954) set to music for the song known as the Negro National Anthem.[10]

LIFT EV'RY VOICE AND SING

*Lift ev'ry voice and sing,*
*Till earth and heaven ring,*
*Ring with the harmonies of liberty;*

*Let our rejoicing rise*
*High as the list'ning skies,*
*Let it resound loud as the rolling sea.*
*Sing a song full of the faith*
*That the dark past has taught us;*
*Sing a song full of the hope*
*That the present has brought us;*
*Facing the rising sun of our new day begun,*
*Let us march on till victory is won.*

*Stony the road we trod,*
*Bitter the chast'ning rod,*
*Felt in the days when hope unborn had died;*
*Yet with a steady beat,*
*Have not our weary feet*
*Come to the place for which our fathers sighed?*
*We have come over a way*
*That with tears has been watered;*
*We have come, treading our path*
*Thru the blood of the slaughtered,*
*Out from the gloomy past,*
*Till now we stand at last*
*Where the white gleam of our*
*Bright star is cast.*

*God of our weary years,*
*God of our silent tears,*
*Thou who hast brought us*
*Thus far on the way;*

*Thou who hast by Thy might,*
*Led us into the light,*
*Keep us forever in the path we pray.*
*Lest our feet stray from the places,*
*Our God, where we met Thee,*
*Lest our hearts, drunk*
*With the wine of the world, we forget Thee;*
*Shadowed beneath Thy hand,*
*May we forever stand,*
*True to our God,*
*True to our native land.*

THOUGH MINDFUL OF how stony the road to equal protection remained in our country, African Americans disagreed on the method and pace of removing the stones. Followers of educator Booker T. Washington accepted his proposed compromise: compassion and patience while segregation slowly died. Supporters of intellectual heavyweight William Edward Burghardt (commonly known as W.E.B.) Du Bois (1868–1963) preferred assertiveness, legal action, and integration, as did militant entrepreneur William Henry Trotter (1872–1934) and investigative journalist Ida B. Wells-Barnett (1852–1931).

Considered "a credit to his race," Washington spoke at the 1895 Cotton States and International Exposition, a fair held in Atlanta to promote trade between the South and countries in Central and South America. The first African American to address an integrated audience in the South, Washington appeared to chide colored people for seeking, and indeed gaining, political access during Reconstruction instead of pursuing an industrial or vocational education as a means to self-sufficiency.

Washington's speech was dubbed "The Atlanta Compromise" because in challenging whites to support efforts that would help Negroes realize their full potential, he assured them Negroes would remain as loyal, patient, and law-abiding as they had been in the past. Bringing the speech to a close, he declared, "In all things that are purely social, we can be as separate as the fingers, yet one as the hand in all things essential to mutual progress."

Although using the hand was an excellent visual aid, all the fingers are actually connected, and the phrase "all things essential to mutual progress" could mean equal access to education, employment, libraries, medical care, and public accommodations, to name a few. But Negroes did not have equal access to any of these nationwide, which is why the three aforementioned activists publicly denounced Washington's proposal. Again, time and space allow only a brief mention of their contributions to the quest for African-Americans' civil rights.

W.E.B. Du Bois, the first African-American to receive a doctorate degree from Harvard University, saw a liberal arts education not only as the means to professional and financial security, but also as ammunition in courtroom battles for civil rights. Renowned as an author, sociologist, and co-founder of the NAACP, Du Bois urged the federal government to dismantle Jim

Crow nationwide. Disenchanted by the pace of both the government and the NAACP, he cancelled his membership with the latter, renounced his citizenship with the former, and moved to Accra, Ghana, in 1961. Fortunately, he left *The Souls of Black Folk* and *The Gift of Black Folk*—accounts of the often overlooked roles African Americans played in the growth and development of our country.

Like Du Bois, William Henry Trotter favored a liberal arts education, and he adamantly opposed Washington's conciliatory proposal. Determined to discredit any movement suggesting Negroes accept segregation or move slowly in their quest for economic, political, and social justice, he and twenty-eight African American business owners, ministers, and teachers formed the Niagara Movement (1905–1909), the first black civil rights organization. The group demanded an end to all forms of racial discrimination, including voting rights, health care, housing, and education.

Possibly the African American woman most openly critical of Washington, Ida B. Wells-Barnett was a co-founder of the NAACP, as well as an educator, journalist, and activist. She is recognized for promoting women's right to vote, equal educational opportunity, and equal protection, particularly the passage of anti-lynching legislation. Documented cases of lynching between 1882 and 1968 stand at 4,743: 3,446 blacks, 1,297 whites. Mississippi ranks first with 581, followed by Georgia's 531, and Texas's 493.[11]

In 1892, Wells-Barnett denounced the lynching of three colored grocers in Memphis. Writing for the *Memphis Free Press,* which she co-owned, Wells-Barnett spoke openly about the power of white women who might falsely accuse Negro men who rejected their advances. Although rape ranked third—after homicide and other causes—in lynching cases, it seems whites assumed most Negro men who were lynched had indeed raped white women.[12] But Barnett spoke the truth. For example, one of my friend's ancestors, who had been taught to read and write for his job, was lynched for teaching his children. And except for quick thinking, her father would have been falsely accused of rape and hanged. A bellman in Texas, he was ordered to disrobe after delivering luggage to a white woman's room. Startled, he heard her say, "If you don't, I'll scream rape and you'll be hung." Thinking on his feet, he assured her that as soon as he reported back to the lobby—so as not to cause alarm—he would return. But instead of the lobby, he ran to the railroad, hopped into a boxcar, and prayed until the train arrived in Chicago.

Fortunately Wells-Barnett was out of town when the article was printed. In retaliation, white mobs destroyed the *Memphis Free Press*'s office and threatened to lynch her if she returned to Memphis. After making Chicago her home, Wells-Barnett continued her crusade against lynching, her fights for women's right to vote, and her advocacy for integrated public schools.

Taking the baton from Wells-Barnett, multilingual Paul Robeson (1898–1976) used his bass-baritone voice to promote immediate action against injustice everywhere. Addressing the United Nations, he accused the United States of genocide for failing to pass anti-lynching legislation. In concerts, he sang songs of freedom, Negro spirituals, and folk songs, often singing in the audience's native language. Unable to visit Jewish friends he had met on a previous trip to Russia, Robeson sang in Yiddish. At rallies, he urged Negroes to reach out not only to the less fortunate in America but also to their fellowmen bound by European colonialism in Africa, the Caribbean Islands, India—worldwide.

A. Phillip Randolph (1889–1979) seconded Robeson's motion for prompt action against discrimination. A college graduate, Randolph worked as a porter and an elevator operator. His experience on the railway compelled him to meet with other Negro porters and form the Brotherhood of Sleeping Car Porters, the first Negro labor union. After securing an agreement that improved working conditions on the railway, Randolph planned a march on Washington to protest discrimination in employment nationwide.

News of the march got President Roosevelt's attention, causing him to issue Executive Order 8802 (June 25, 1941), which banned discriminatory employment practices in the United States's defense industry. Randolph canceled the march, but he was not done yet. After he organized the League for Nonviolent Civil Disobedience Against Military Segregation, President Truman signed Executive Order 9981 (July 26, 1948), which established the President's Committee on Equality of Treatment and Opportunity in the Armed Services, thereby desegregating the military.

When it came to education, no one did more to desegregate the curriculum in public schools than historian Carter Godwin Woodson (1875–1950). Born to enslaved African parents, Woodson had little formal education before he was twenty. But in eight years, he received his high school diploma, a teaching certificate, and a college degree. The second African American to earn a PhD from Harvard University, Woodson has been called the "Father of African American History."[13] To rectify what he called "mis-education," Woodson campaigned for the inclusion of Negro History in public schools. His campaign ended in 1926, with the second week of February designated as Negro History Week. Although this week was chosen to honor the birthdays of Frederick Douglass and Abraham Lincoln, Douglass's autobiography indicates his birthdate as unknown, but February 14th is recognized as the day.

IF AFRICAN AMERICAN history textbooks existed in 1926, they were depleted before I started school in dinosaur days. The curriculum at my grade school and high school included

biographies of abolitionists Frederick Douglass, Harriett Tubman, and Sojourner Truth, who was also a women's activist;
educators Mary McLeod Bethune and Booker T. Washington;
scientist George Washington Carver; the literary works of
Phyllis Wheatley, Paul Laurence Dunbar, and James Weldon
Johnson; and cosmetologist-entrepreneur Madame C. J. Walker.
In Negro communities, parents and teachers supplemented the
curriculum with oral African American history and folklore.

Since 1976, public schools throughout the country have
observed the entire month of February as African American
History Month. Today, books about African Americans' culture and their contributions to the world, written by both
black and white authors, are available for inclusion in the study
of our country's history throughout the school year.

♫ *Accompaniments* ♫

*Haunted by a photo of a hanging (a Negro who had been
lynched), English teacher Robert Meeropol (1903–1986),
wrote the poem "Strange Fruit" in 1937. He later set it to
music. Although lynching is not mentioned, the message is
quite clear, especially in Billie Holiday's rendition, which
was first recorded in 1939. Named* TIME *magazine's song
of the century in 1999, "Strange Fruit" is also in the National
Recording Registry.*

*Despite political discord, "Come Sunday" was the common
plea of African Americans during the time captured in this
chapter. And Mahalia Jackson's vocals are the best. Duke
Ellington, who some consider the greatest jazz composer*

*and bandleader of his time, composed the piece as the first movement of the suite "Black, Brown, and Beige," which he performed at Carnegie Hall in 1943. Nat King Cole's rendition of Thomas "Fats" Waller and Mike Jackson's "Beale Street Blues" speaks volumes about one side of the times not presented in this chapter. I like W.C. Handy's instrumental version. "Weary Blues," as performed by Duke Ellington and Johnny Hodges, is not at all weary. Like the poem, it is a moving picture of an incident in one man's life during the Harlem Renaissance.*

*Unlike the equal access most Americans have today, the African American activists, artists, doctors, entrepreneurs, and scientists who are briefly discussed herein were subjected to all kinds of prejudice. Yet, innovative as ever, these men and women found the means to complete their professional training, conduct research, and build their own hospitals and nursing schools, as well as their own businesses.*

*For example, after earning his master's degree at Harvard, Percy Julian applied for an assistantship, a requirement for the doctoral program he planned to pursue. The university rejected his application and the subsequent one for admission to its doctoral program. If Julian's application for an assistantship had been accepted, he would have taught part-time or conducted research at the university. However, many of the major universities did not offer assistantships to Negroes because of their concern that white students would not accept colored instructors. Julian satisfied his yearning for further studies by traveling to Austria where he earned his PhD in chemistry from the University of Vienna.*

*But when Julian returned to America, he faced discrimination yet again. Because many firms did not hire Negro executives out of fear that white employees would not follow their direction, it was virtually impossible for Julian to find* *a position that merited his higher education. He applied at the Institute of Paper Chemistry in Appleton, Wisconsin, but the company could not hire him because a statute prohibited Negroes from spending even a night in the city. He was then rejected by DuPont because the hiring team did not know he was a Negro when the offer was made. Eventually, Julian accepted the position of chief chemist at the Glidden Company (1936–1954). In 1954, Julian founded Julian Laboratories, Inc., with facilities in the United States and Mexico. He also had a chemical plant in Guatemala. In 1961, he sold the lab in Mexico to pharmaceutical giant Smith Kline and French for $2.3 million. The company is now GlaxoSmithKline. The Upjohn Company bought the plant in Guatemala.*

*The daughter of former slaves who died when she was a child, Sarah Breedlove McWilliams (1867–1919) used herself as a guinea pig to experiment with secret ingredients that to her surprise not only stopped her hair loss, but also stimulated its growth. She then formed her own company to sell the product door to door. Later, she added cosmetics and other hair-care products for colored women. In 1906, she married Charles Joseph Walker and became known as Madame "C.J." Walker. Although her business grew in her adopted hometown of Denver, she moved to Pittsburgh before building her headquarters in Indianapolis in 1910.*

*Walker's success in business was matched by her generosity and advocacy for civil rights. In 1911, she contributed $1,000 to the YMCA's building fund in Indianapolis; she contributed scholarships for students at black colleges, gave financial support to orphanages, retirement homes, and the fund to preserve Frederick Douglass's home in Washington, D.C. She also gave $5,000 to the NAACP to support its anti-lynching campaign in 1919.*

*The property she purchased in downtown Indianapolis in 1919 became the Madame Walker Theatre Center in 1927. The center and Villa Lewaro, her mansion in Irvington, New York, are both national historic landmarks. According to Guinness World Records, Madame C.J. Walker was the first self-made woman millionaire!*

*Now fast-forwarding to modern times . . .*

*At Stanford University Medical Center in 1961, Dr. Samuel Koontz (1930–1981) assisted Dr. Roy Cohn (1910–1989) in performing the first kidney transplant between relatives who were not identical twins—a mother to her daughter. Quite an accomplishment for a man who, in 1948, failed the entrance exam to Arkansas A&M College! After an ambitious appeal to the college's president, Koontz was admitted. With a major in chemistry, he graduated third in his class. Fulfilling his vow to make the college proud by becoming his best as a physician, he received his medical degree from the University of Arkansas Medical School; he then completed his internship and residency at Stanford Service in San Francisco.*

*Dr. Koontz is credited with discovering the anti-rejection property of high doses of methylprednisolone and the benefit of early re-implantation: transplanting another kidney at the earliest sign of rejection. He also worked with the group of researchers who perfected the machine that keeps a kidney viable for up to fifty hours outside the body. In 1976, while on a teaching engagement in South Africa, Dr. Koontz contracted a neurological disorder that was still undiagnosed when he died in December, 1981. At that time, he had performed a world record of over 500 kidney transplants, one on live TV, NBC's Today Show in 1976, prompting over 20,000 people to call in and offer organ donations.*

# Paths to
# Mississippi

$\mathcal{A}$fter the Civil War, many plantation owners were hard-pressed to restore their war-ravaged farms. They lacked the money to hire laborers to plant and harvest crops, could not pay their mortgages, and had no human collateral to secure loans to purchase the supplies and equipment needed to make their land again profitable. To avoid foreclosure on their property, some owners divided their plantations into small parcels, which they leased as quasi-independent farms to Negroes and poor whites. Instead of charging rent and paying wages, the owner shared the crops that he and the lessees produced. From this arrangement came the term "sharecropper."[1] In Mississippi, "tenant farmers" had a similar arrangement: in exchange for lodging, they paid for using the land either with cash, labor, or a portion of their products. Like my earliest identifiable ancestors may have done, some Negroes probably worked on their former slaveholder's plantation.

According to the 1870 United States federal census, my maternal great-grandparents Emanuel (c.1812–?) and Mary Johnson (c.1820–?) are among thirty-six black laborers listed with Manford Walters, a white man, in Township Eight of Jefferson County, Mississippi. With six children ranging from one to seventeen years of age at the beginning of the Civil War, Emanuel and Mary probably remained on Walter's plantation during the war and stayed as sharecroppers afterward. A note here: Judging by his last name, grandfather Emanuel kept the name of a former slaveholder. Of course, if Walters was grandfather's "master," he may have been a Johnson descendant himself who inherited my great-grandparents, or he could have married one who inherited them.

My paternal great-grandparents Boucher (c.1810–?) and Vina Blocker (1826–?) remained on the plantation of their former slaveholder James Henderson, probably as tenant farmers. Based on my immediate family's experience, in exchange for housing, nominal daily wages, and a year-end settlement, Grandfather Boucher and his family would have provided labor for a variety of jobs, including cultivating land, planting and harvesting crops, gardening, maintaining equipment, and managing livestock. For clothing and household goods, they would have shopped at a general store, which Henderson may have owned. If the purchases exceeded their weekly pay, which was based on the number of days worked, the balance would have been charged to their account, just as we do today by using a credit card and paying for our purchases when we receive the bill the following month. If my great-grandparents were short of cash and the general store did not stock a particular item, they would have borrowed money from the plantation owner and purchased the merchandise in a nearby town.

My great-grandparents would have received an annual settlement based on the plantation owner's year-end profits. The settlement was the difference between their share of the year-end profits and the total of what they owed the plantation owner. If the sum of money borrowed and the balance on their account exceeded the settlement, the negative difference was carried over to the next year, a practice that could have created a revolving cycle of debt. I do not know if this was the case with my great-grandparents. But, from my family's experience in Swan Lake, I know this cycle could only be avoided by not borrowing money or charging anything at the general store, which was impossible to do most of the time.

Theoretically, skilled craftsmen were less likely to be debt-ridden because they could design and make some of their own furnishings, such as beds, chairs, benches, tables, and stools. However, their earnings were limited because Black Codes restricted Negroes from competing with whites in trades such as carpentry, masonry, painting, etc. Yet, some skilled tradesmen, including Cousin Steve Powell (1888–1963) prevailed.

During the early 1900s, Cousin Steve was known as the most skillful machinist in Clarksdale, Mississippi. Employed as a millwright at the local cotton mill, he was responsible for keeping the machinery running properly. Having inherited the Powells' mechanical aptitude, he was adept at repairing equipment with intricate parts that required precise eye-hand coordination.

After he restored one of the mill's most complicated machines, his manager called him into the office and said, "Steve, you deserve a promotion. You're the best machinist I've ever had, but I ain't never had a nigger foreman."

Putting on the mask, Cousin Steve thought, *And I've never been called a nigger to my face.* To him, the mispronunciation of Negro meant a trifling, ignorant good-for-nothing, which he certainly was not. Perhaps his manager did not know he was using an offensive term in the Negroes' vernacular.

Despite the mask, my ancestors never lost sight of a brighter future for their children and successive generations. A beneficiary of that future, I peeked into their lives and reconstructed their circuitous paths to Mississippi, where slaveholders brought most of them. The sources for my reconstruction included DNA analyses, given and surnames, two slave ships, slave schedules, and censuses. Following the trail may be challenging, but I hope you will find the twists and turns as enlightening as I did.

BASED ON MY DNA analysis, the path began in the plains of northeast Africa, where my earliest female ancestor lived in 80,000 B.C. From there, it split into three routes: southwest, northwest, and southeast. My paternal great-grandfather's given name, Boucher, indicates the northwest trail included a stop in England. The French word for butcher, *boucher*, is also a surname in Lincolnshire, England, an area settled by the French after the Norman Conquest in 1066 and identified as one of the places in the British Isles inhabited by people who have genes that match some of mine.

In the 1750s, a British captain named Edward Boucher spent a lot of time in Africa purchasing children, men, and women whom he transported to Charleston, South Carolina. Research on Captain Boucher's voyages to the Americas suggests one of Grandfather Boucher's ancestors may have been in the hold on either the *Fortune* or the *Sylvia*, probably as a child or young adult.

With Captain Boucher at the helm and twenty-five crew members on board, the eighty-ton *Fortune* departed from Bristol, England, on February 2, 1753. Neither the date of arrival in Africa, nor the date of departure for America is shown. However, the *Fortune* docked in Charleston, South Carolina, on June 26, 1754, which indicates it took over a year for Captain Boucher to complete his transactions in Africa. Of course, some of the time would have been spent maintaining the ship, securing supplies, and recruiting African translators. (Note: Raw data on slave ships were found online at slavevoyages.org.)

According to the *Fortune*'s records, the first purchases were made in Sierra Leone, the second at the Windward Coast, and the third on the Gold Coast, the principal place of purchase. Captain Boucher departed from Africa with 208 slaves: 14.9 percent men, 13.1 percent women, 41.7 percent boys, and 30.4 percent girls. One hundred eighty Africans arrived in Charleston but only 168 disembarked, which indicates twenty-eight died on the Middle Passage and were buried at sea. Twelve apparently died without being discovered until after the ship docked in South Carolina.

Captain Boucher's next two voyages were on the *Sylvia*. On February 2, 1756, he left Bristol, England, for the Gambia, where he planned to purchase and deliver 150 Africans to South Carolina. On April 7, 1756, he began trading goods from Great Britain for Africans in Senegambia and offshore Atlantic. He departed from Senegambia with 230 Africans, eighty more than planned, and arrived in Charleston with 197 on September 1, 1756. Thirty-three did not survive the Middle Passage.

The time spent in Africa and the date of departure are not shown, but allowing four weeks to travel from England to Africa, one can calculate mid-May as the arrival date, allow about a month of bartering in Africa, and estimate late June as the departure date, which would leave about nine weeks to cross the Middle Passage, the average length of the voyage.

The *Sylvia* departed on its second trip to Africa on October 13, 1757. Trading for 200 Africans began in Gambia on November 11, 1757. On April 24, 1758, Captain Boucher departed from Senegambia with 205 Africans. Nine weeks later, on July 1, he arrived in South Carolina and docked at Sullivan's Island with 160, a loss of forty-five on the Middle Passage. Boucher departed from Charleston on August 15, 1758, and as far as I can determine, he never returned to North America.

To date, I have found neither data that specify when, where, or how Boucher Blocker's family arrived in South Carolina nor any records of Boucher slaveholders in that area. This leads me to speculate that an African from the *Fortune* or the *Sylvia* was sold as "one of Boucher's" and given the name Boucher, which was passed down through two or three generations, ending with my great-grandfather. Speculating about my African ancestry is yet another lingering effect of slavery.

Considering the length of time the captain spent in Africa and the French Boucher's settling in Lincolnshire, England—the area linked to the captain's surname—I wonder if it is merely a coincidence, or if there is a biological connection between my great-grandfather's first name and the captain's last name. The answer, I am afraid, is enclosed with someone's skeletal remains. Like Shakespeare said in his play *Julius Caesar*: "The evil that men do lives after them: the good is oft interred with their bones."

The third and final leg of my ancestors' paths to Mississippi began when the slaveholding Blocker, Brown, Johnson, Powell, Henderson, McMullen, and Smith families migrated from Virginia and South Carolina to Mississippi and Tennessee. The Blockers and Powells are my paternal ancestors; the Browns, Johnsons, McMullins/McMullens, and Smiths maternal. From United States federal censuses, slave records, and Boucher's date and place of birth, it appears that he or his ancestors were sold to a Blocker slaveholder in South Carolina. Of five South Carolinian Blockers identified as slaveholders, Sarah, D.L., Nancy, and J.M. Blocker were the most likely ones. Sarah was born in 1783, D.L. in 1790, Nancy in 1798, and J.M. in 1799. If they are siblings, and if their parents were slaveholders who willed slaves to them, Nancy may have inherited Boucher: the 1850 slave schedule shows her as the owner of five male slaves, ranging from age twenty-three to thirty. I believe Boucher to be the thirty-year-old who was later sold.

The 1860 federal census slave schedules list eighty slaves residing in Mississippi with slaveholder James Henderson who, like Boucher, was born in South Carolina. The slaves' names are not shown, but using age, race, and gender, I tentatively identified Boucher, his wife Vina, and their son Winfield: Boucher is listed as a forty-year-old black male, Vina as a thirty-five-year-old black female, and Winfield as a fifteen-year-old male. Later, I found Boucher identified as one of Henderson's laborers, which gives a touch of credence to my conclusion that he was sold: had he been born on Henderson's farm, his surname would have been Henderson.

On the 1870 census, my grandfather Winfield Blocker (1845–c.1930) is one of thirty-five laborers on Lemuel Henderson's farm in Mississippi. (Also born in South Carolina, Lemuel may have been James's brother.) At the age of twenty-five, Winfield and his first wife, twenty-five-year-old Martha (1846–?) have two children: three-year-old William and one-year-old Rosetta.

By 1880, the family has grown to eight with the addition of Vina, Winfield, Arnella, and Sweetie. I think Sweetie is a nickname, and Vina is named after her grandmother. Listed on the census with their place of birth shown as South Carolina and North Carolina respectively, Boucher and Vina Blocker live on the Henderson Plantation in Hinds County, Mississippi. Winfield, his wife Martha, and their six children live in Dry Grove, an area in Hinds.

Unfortunately, a fire destroyed most of the 1890 census,

but the 1900 census shows Winfield's birth year as 1851. This report shows he has been married to his second wife Mattie Powell (1874–?) for seven years. Winfield is forty-nine, while Mattie is a young twenty-six. Ethel, Christianna, Olivia, Maydee, and my father Claude are listed as their children.

Identified as the mother of three children, Mattie is clearly Ethel and Christianna's stepmother, who by their ages, fourteen and twelve respectively, must be the last two children from Winfield's first marriage. Olivia and Maydee are my father's sisters. I know of Aunt Olivia from oral family history; I knew Maydee as my aunt Mamie. Either her name was misspelled on the census, or Mamie was her nickname.

Aunt Olivia, known by her pet name Ollie, was said to have been quite particular. Cousin Rose spoke of how she carefully applied her makeup before going to work, immediately changed from her work clothes when she came home, freshened up and gently cleansed her face before dinner, then lightly reapplied her makeup before retiring for the evening. Cousin Rose and my sister Nellie told me, "You are just like your aunt Ollie." They said that not because of physical features, but because I was a neatnik too. According to my middle- and high-school classmate Zadie Marie, at the end of the day, I left school looking like I had just arrived—not a hair out of place, no ink stains or pencil marks on my dress, and not a speck of dirt on my white penny loafers. But I digress . . .

Now, where was I?

Oh yes, continuing my research on Grandfather Winfield, I found South Carolina as his father's place of birth on the 1900, 1910, and 1920 United States federal censuses. This is the same place of birth shown for Great-Grandfather Boucher on the 1870 and 1880 censuses. Although Winfield's age is different on each census after 1880, and he has a younger wife—a common practice at that time—he is about ninety on the 1930 federal census. Thus, he was born around 1845 as shown on the 1870 census, where I found him first.

On the 1920 census, Winfield's birthdate is recorded as 1854—again the last two digits in his birth year are transposed—and he is married to his third wife, Laura. She is thirty-seven, he is sixty-six, and they have three children: Annie, Luella, and George. By 1930, Winfield and Laura have parted ways. At the age of ninety, he is living with Jim and Christine Jones—identified as "father-in-law," he is obviously Christine's father—and she is Christiana, whose name was misspelled on the 1900 census.

With the exception of his first wife, Martha, who was the same age as he, my grandfather's history indicates he preferred younger women. The discrepancies in his age are probably the result of poor record keeping, compromised memories, and the tendency to estimate the age of Negroes, especially those who were slaves for whom birth certificates were not issued. After examining several federal censuses and related documents to identify Winfield's family and reviewing my notes with a genealogical researcher, I believe the pieces on this side of my paternal family's puzzle are where they belong.

WHILE THE PATERNAL line of my father's family tree can be traced to South Carolina fairly accurately, the maternal line has missing branches. I do know, however, that the roots extend to Virginia. Census data for his mother, Mattie (1874–?), show that her father, Henry Powell (c.1835–?), was born in Virginia. A comparison of oral family history with my research suggests he and his brother James were separated during slavery and reunited in Hinds County, Mississippi, after the Civil War.

During the separation, Henry may have lived in Alabama before settling in Mississippi and marrying Jennie, whose first name is the only information I have about her.

Because Powell is a rather common surname with a variety of spellings, this section of my paternal family's puzzle has missing pieces. But my DNA analyses appear to have found one more. Several weeks after being shocked senseless by my European ancestry, I received an email from a man who indicated the analysis of his DNA at Ancestry.com showed a 96 percent degree of certainty that he and I are fifth to sixth cousins. When I opened the attachment to his email and looked at the photos on his family tree, I discovered that he and all his relatives are melanin-poor, while I am melanin-rich. Oh, dear!

Right away I answered him, offering the surnames in my family and the states where my ancestors were born, adding that I did not look like any of his relatives. Not to be daunted, he wrote back, emphasizing his intent to continue researching his family's roots with the expectation of identifying our common ancestor. Two years later, when our DNA analyses by 23andMe confirmed we were cousins, I sent him an email to ascertain if he had identified any of his ancestors who were slaveholders.

Again, I shared my ancestors' surnames and places of birth. And sure enough, one of this man's Powell great-grandfathers, several generations removed, lived in Virginia during the 1700s! The only acceptable explanation for our matching genes is that this Powell, one of his offspring, or a relative had a star-crossed love affair with one of my female African ancestors. Interestingly, the man who contacted me is an engineer: mechanical aptitude runs in the Powell side of our family (remember Cousin Steve?).

Now for Mother's lineage, my earliest identifiable ancestors.

✐

ACCORDING TO THE 1880 federal census, Great-Grandfather
Emanuel Johnson's father was born in Virginia, his mother in
South Carolina. Their names and ages are not shown, but
Grandfather Emanuel's age indicates his parents were born in
the mid to late 1700s. Considering their last name and states of
birth, it seems safe to assume that they were purchased by a
Johnson slaveholding family.

In 1830, a Jas (James) Johnson lived in Culpepper, Vir-
ginia, with his parents and three siblings. On the 1840 census,
James, his family, and their fifty-six slaves live in Mississippi.
Tentatively identified by age and gender, two of those slaves
were Emanuel and his wife Mary. Their identities were confirmed on the 1870 census, which shows both were born in
Mississippi. Their six children are listed as Fredie, Troy, Kate,
James, Mack—my mother's father—and Emanel. It appears the
census taker misspelled Emanel and Fredie (Freddie or
Freddy). On *Mississippi Marriages 1776–1935,* the name is
spelled Emanuel, and his marriage to Mary Jane Smith is
shown as December 29, 1882. Of course, this is merely the date
their jumping the broom was officially recorded.

Mother spelled her maternal grandparents' names as Len
and Katherine McMullin, not Lew and Kate McMullen as
shown on the 1880 federal census. (Kate is a short name for
Katherine, and the "n" in Len could have been mistaken for a
"w.") Despite the misspelling of their names, based on the brief
family history Mother sent me in the early 1980s, I am certain
these are her grandparents. In addition, Grandmother Harriett
and her sister Matilda are included with Lew and Kate's children: Charity, Caroline, Haley, Harriett, and Tilda/Matilda. By
1910, the family includes Susan, Savanna, Gira, Earnest,

Lenard, and William. Kate is listed as a sixty-year-old widow, so four-year-old Lenard and ten-year-old Earnest are probably her grandsons.

In *Mississippi Marriages, 1776–1935*, I found Grandmother listed as Cate Brown and Grandfather as Lem McMullen. Obviously, they "jumped the broom" years before their marriage was legally recorded on January 28, 1867—more than likely, courtesy of the Freedmen's Bureau.

Len was born around 1825 in Tennessee, and Katherine, about 1844 in Mississippi. Their dates of birth indicate they were slaves, and from the 1850 federal census, I deduce Len was purchased by a McMullen slaveholder, possibly Cullen. Born in North Carolina around 1794, Cullen McMullen migrated to Tennessee before the birth of his son in 1828.

The 1830 Census shows twenty-four slaves residing with McMullen in Carroll, Tennessee. Grandfather Len's date of birth indicates he is one of the seven male slaves listed under the age of ten. From Tennessee, McMullen moved to Mississippi, where he and his forty-nine slaves lived in 1840.

Skipping to the 1880 census, I found Grandmother Katherine's occupation listed as a housekeeper. Obviously, she was a house servant because there were no African stay-at-home moms.

In 1896, Len and Katherine's daughter Harriett (1871–?) married Mack Johnson (1860–?). The couple had four children: one son, B J, and three girls, Nellia, Kathleen Christine, and Lula, my mother.

Grandmother Harriett died before I was born, but I knew her younger sister Matilda. According to Mother, Grandmother Harriet was an "Indian," the term for Native Americans during dinosaur days. Although one's ancestry cannot be determined by physical features alone, except the few of us with milk chocolate complexions, neither Mother nor any of her children had any discernible Native American features. Only one of my DNA analyses shows a trace (0.4%) of Native American and Asian ancestry. But, Aunt Matilda looked like she had more.

With high cheekbones and black, wavy hair styled in two braids that hung down her back, Aunt Matilda did not look or act like any of us. While we were caramel to dark chocolate and somewhat lively, she was fair and rather reserved, always sitting quietly and staring straight ahead, her eyes filled with peaceful sadness and sorrowful resignation. I do not remember ever seeing her smile, but her demeanor touched the best part of me. Sitting beside her on the porch while she gently swayed back and forth in her rocking chair was enough fun for me. I would sit there until the cicadae signaled it was time for Mother and me to go home. Of course, I took my time getting ready to leave because Cousin Kate, Aunt Matilda's albino daughter, was left-handed like I am, and she treated me like I was as grown-up as she.

Unlike Cousin Kate, who never married, Grandmother Harriett seems to have preferred marriage. By the time Mother reached puberty, she had learned to keep enough space between herself and her second stepfather to avoid his unruly hands. Angered by her rebuffs, he tried to ration her food, telling Grandmother Harriett, "Don't put nothing else on that gal's plate. She eat too much anyway."

Mother said, "He was so mean and lowdown!" Feeling unsafe around him, she decided to marry the first man who proposed, vowing to never subject her children to a stepfather. Considering her situation, I imagine when Daddy asked, "Will you . . .," Mother said, "Yes!"

Which brings me to their paths to Swan Lake.

The Blockers and Johnsons worked as tenant farmers near Jackson, Mississippi. If work was not profitable on one farm, they moved to another. Both families migrated north from Jackson (Desoto, Hinds, and LeFlor counties) to Swan Lake (Tallahatchie county) in the early 1900s.

Like children often did, my father worked in the fields with his parents instead of going to school because his parents needed as many hands in the field as possible. With him, his two older sisters, and a younger brother working alongside them, they could earn enough to pay for their purchases at the general store instead of buying on credit. Thus, they would receive a larger settlement in the fall and avoid becoming trapped by a revolving cycle of debt.

Daddy used to see Mother as she walked to school, past the field where he and his parents worked. After their wedding, he told her how he would boast to his friends, "You see that little short girl with the pretty legs? One day, I am going to make her my wife."

They were married on December 8, 1918.

All was well between them until it was time to join a church. Mother chose Bethlehem Missionary Baptist Church, but because Daddy wanted to help build its membership, he preferred the newer St. Able. Equally firm in their convictions, Mother joined Bethlehem, took the children with her, and became an usher; but Daddy thought it would not "look right" for him to attend one church while his wife and children were members of another, so he did not join or attend either one.

With his mechanical aptitude, Daddy was an engineer, chemist, carpenter, mechanic, and architect all rolled into one. He could build anything: barns, wagons, buggies, houses, troughs, fences, and even outhouses. A good mechanic, Daddy knew how to repair farm equipment, cars, trucks, and almost anything with a motor. He also made toys for his children, their favorite being the men he sculpted from wood. A long stick with a ball carved at the end was attached to the figures. When the men were tapped on the head with the ball, they crossed their legs and danced.

For fun, Daddy loved to umpire baseball games, play his guitar, collect records, and listen to music. I was told he prided himself on being the first to buy new records for his collection of blues and jazz. Like Daddy, I collect all kinds of music. Mother often said to me, "You're just like your father's people." I didn't know what she meant until I met Cousin Rose, the first college graduate in her immediate family, like I was in mine, and a lover of fine music too.

A dapper dresser, Daddy did not like wearing a tie, but he loved vests and hats. He was also a good provider, always making sure his children had plenty of food and homemade toys. He canned vegetables and stored sweet potatoes so the family would have enough for the winter. And oh how he loved a neat house and cleanly swept yard!

To hear my sister Nellie tell it, Daddy was an amateur pharmacist and medicine man too. He would burn sugar, add a little corn whiskey and molasses, and blend them to make a syrup. When the children had a fever or caught a cold, he gave them a teaspoon of the syrup, put them in bed, and covered them with heavy quilts to reduce the fever. The next morning, they woke up feeling like new!

As a tenant farmer on the Flautt Plantation—in addition to plowing, planting, and harvesting crops—Daddy managed the livestock and took care of the equipment. According to oral family history, Daddy was a proud and courageous man who would not allow anyone to mistreat him or his children.

My siblings often played with the Flautt children, usually in their house or yard. One day, my eldest brothers Willie and Fred came home in tears. When Daddy asked why they were crying, Fred told him the Flautts' younger son Billy had hit them. Daddy asked if they hit him back. "No sir," Fred said.

He told them, "Turn around, go on back down there, and hit him back, as hard as he hit you, and don't come home 'til you do."

They ran back, called Billy to come outside, and gave him the last fight he had with them.

Now, this happened in the 1920s when colored people, regardless of their age, were expected to be subservient to all whites, including young children. Negroes could be burned, mutilated, and hanged for breaking a Jim Crow law, such as "being uppity" and not saying "yes, sir" when answering a white man, looking directly at a white person instead of to the side, or touching a white person's hand when picking up change from a counter.

Of course, Daddy knew this, and he was well aware of Swan Lake's hanging tree, but none of that stopped him from teaching his sons to defend themselves. With his reputation as a reliable laborer and groomer, skilled carpenter, and machinist, Daddy knew the Flautts needed him, which gave him reason to expect them to intervene on his behalf if necessary.

His family an even dozen, before I showed up at 1:15 on a Sunday morning, Daddy told Mother I was the last child they would have—I guess he thought a family of thirteen was enough. Although Daddy died just as I was learning to walk, I remember how he let me play in the trough while he watered the horses. This is my only memory of him, but I do remember Mother telling me how I cried every day at about the time Daddy would have come home. A smart lady, she thought if Sarah took me to the trough just as he had done, I would stop crying—and she said I did.

The other information I have about Daddy is a composite

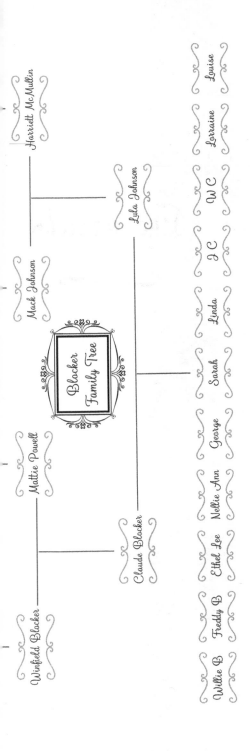

of two of my older sisters' recollections. Because of poor vision, Sarah dictated hers to me during the summer of 2003. Nellie wrote hers in a letter to me on September 27, 2003, a mere three and a half months before she died. What a gift that was to me, and I hope to Lamin too!

## ♫ Accompaniments ♫

◎

*Oh, the times I have yearned for "My Father's Eyes!" And how Daddy would have enjoyed B.B. King and Eric Clapton's rendition of his number-one blues favorite, "Worried Life Blues!" My mind's eye can even see his feet a-patting as Nina Simone takes on "Trouble in Mind." Now, Mother was not the blues or rock and roll type, but she did admit to enjoying Sonny Boy Williamson. A funny storyteller herself, she probably liked his song "The Hunt." I imagine his hot harmonica jamming got her attention too.*

Pi

Boucher
Blacker — Vina    Henry
Powell    Jennie    Emmanuel
Johnson    Mary Jane
Smith    Len
Mc Mullin    Katherine
Brown

*To put faces on the places and on some of the people discussed in this book, I've included a few of my favorite photos in this section. Because there is truth in the adage, a picture is worth a thousand words, I used fewer than that with the snapshots of my immediate family members and those of three individuals who played Oscar-worthy supporting roles in my life. The anecdotes about my siblings are based on obituaries, oral family history, and my experience with them.*

*With two to three years between the birth of each of my five brothers and five sisters, we grew up in sets. The first set, my four eldest siblings, had moved away from home before I was born. Three were married, one was single. The three middle siblings were teenagers by the time I learned to talk, and the last set of four consisted of my brothers J C and W C, my sister Lorraine (nee Ruth Lorean), and me.*

Mother and Daddy had never taken any pictures together, but she changed that when she returned to Memphis after celebrating her 79th birthday at my home in Santa Monica, California. Ever creative and thoughtful, Mother took the only photo she had of Daddy and a favorite one of herself to a studio to make this portrait for my birthday in 1984. My best present ever!

*Claude Blocker: c. July 1898–August 8, 1943*
*Lula J. Blocker: c. September 1, 1902–May 13, 1991*

*2018 Blocker Family Census*
*2 children, 56 grandchildren, 185 great-grandchildren,*
*259 great-great-grandchildren, 34 great-great-great-grandchildren*
*In Memoriam*
*9 children, 12 grandchildren, 5 great-grandchildren, 2 great-great-grandchildren*

My parents' firstborn, Willie B, preferred the name Terry, but we addressed him by his middle name, simply the letter B. After Daddy died, B came back home and assumed the role of male head of household. Multitalented, he taught himself to play the guitar, make home repairs of all kinds, and even cook. When he and his wife Pearl divorced, B requested and was given full custody of their son and two daughters. A devoted father, B loved each child dearly and equally, as his daughters attested at his memorial service on March 30, 1997. How it warmed my heart to hear their accolades!

From his humble beginnings as a tenant farmer's son, B migrated to New York, New York, where his homestyle cooking earned him the position of chef for the Penn Central Transportation Company. After his fill of preparing meals, B worked as a building superintendent in New York until he retired and relocated to Memphis, Tennessee, in the late 1980s.

*W C, J C, Freddy B, and George*

Freddy—yes, the letter B is his middle name too—the second-born, was a man with a mission. After an honorable discharge from the Army, he returned to Swan Lake. But, instead of la-boring in the fields, Fred worked as a clerk at the Flautts' store until he had saved enough money to move. With an interme-diate stop in Clarksdale, Mississippi, he proved his driving skills as a trucker.

A year or two later, he moved to Memphis, Tennessee, where he met and married the love of his life, Mary Alice Moore. He and Alice had three boys. A trucker and an investor in real estate, Fred retired as one of Roadway Transportation Company's safest drivers.

A light snow covered the ground the day of his funeral, December 8, 2002, which was fitting for a seasoned senior with only a few strands of gray. I do miss him, especially his meeting me at the airport on my trips to Memphis!

George, the fifth-born, spoke softly but not hastily, giving his opinion in a sensitive and loving manner. For example, he would say, "Now if it was me, this is what I would do. But that might not be right for you."

Migrating to St. Louis, Missouri, with farming his only experience, George became both physically and emotionally exhausted from working multiple jobs that paid barely enough to support his wife and eleven children. Consequently, his brothers-in-law brought him to live with Mother in Memphis. Although his health was restored, George never recovered from being taken away from his family.

A gentle man, kind brother, and devoted son, George was a favorite uncle too. My heart cries when I think of his leaving us too soon, on November 7, 1992. But, listening to his favorite composition, Grover Washington's "Mr. Magic," puts me in the groove.

J C, the eighth-born, was a great sport who appreciated a good joke, even if the joke was on him. He and his wife Tomizene had six children. To honor our uncle and our father, he adopted the name James Claude. J C boasted about his skills as a trucker, saying he could take a nap while driving and not leave the road, always waking up right in the nick of time.

At least once on the road, he actually did fall asleep . . .

While making a delivery one day, Freddy Jr.—also a trucker— was about to pass a sixteen-wheeler when he looked over and saw the driver gripping the steering wheel, head bowed, fast asleep. Right away, he realized the driver was his uncle J C. Freddy called on his short-wave radio, but J C didn't answer.

So Freddy drove beside the truck and blocked traffic for over twenty minutes while he continued calling. Finally J C answered, looked over, smiled, and kept right on driving.

I was grief stricken when he passed on October 10, 2010, but hearing his hearty chuckle in my mind, I smiled. Thinking of him wearing one of his many caps or hats still brings a smile.

W C, the ninth-born, was known by the name of his favorite candy bar, Nutty, until his late teens. He eventually accepted the name William Clay—which our sister Linda chose for him in the 1960s—but his nieces and nephews affectionately address him as "Uncle Dub."

A resourceful teenager, W C refused to be hampered by Jim Crow when he found employment in Memphis. From his first job as a busboy, he advanced to management positions in the food service industry. During his weekend gigs—whether as a tenor or baritone—he had juke joints jumping in West Memphis, Arkansas, and in nightclubs in Memphis too. According to my niece Bettie Ann, many ladies shouted when he sang a solo at church.

W C retired as supervising chef at Bowles Hospital in Memphis, where he met his wife, Louise Robinson. They became parents of three boys and two girls. After retiring, he became the owner of two Blockers' Soul Food Restaurants: one in Memphis and one in Olive Branch, Mississippi.

Ethel Lee, the third-born, grew to be a gracious, wise, and generous lady. I remember fondly that she was the only sibling who sent money to me while I was in college.

When she found me crying while I was practicing my cursive writing at home to avoid my third-grade classmates' ridicule at school, Ethel encouraged me, saying, "Don't be ashamed of using your left hand, because doing so means you're special. Those children are just jealous because your writing is better than theirs." What a boost to my self-esteem!

To end a star-crossed love affair, Ethel moved to Chicago around 1952. The mother of a daughter and a son, she was mortally wounded in mid-September 1962. Her death was a devastating loss for our entire family.

Nellie Ann, the fourth child, was my most progressive sister. An enterprising woman and a great cook, she and Fred owned a café in Memphis during the 1960s. Her three-flavor pound cake was beyond compare! When she would surprise me with one for my birthday, it was such a treat for me—and for my friends too. Always loving and supportive to our family, Nellie was the only sibling at my high school commencement.

Although her dream of becoming a professional singer was not realized, she sang in the choir at church. Nellie was self-employed as a seamstress, day-care provider, and caregiver. A dedicated daughter, she brought Mother into her home and gave her the best of care for almost two years. She and her husband, Ore Lee Taylor, had seven girls and three boys.

Nellie quietly slipped away from us on January 16, 2004. I

miss her dearly, but I am comforted by my phone visit with her in late December 2003. As our heartfelt conversation came to a close, Nellie exclaimed, "At least I know my baby sister loves me." Indeed, I do!

∽

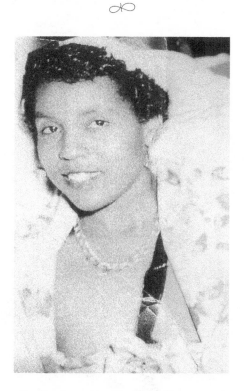

*Sarah on her wedding day, December 25, 1946*

Sarah, the sixth-born, was the family's sweetheart. The mother of four daughters and one son, an avid reader, and another great cook, she sent me the best batch of oatmeal-raisin cookies during my second year of college.

Sarah and her husband Haze Calhoun made Swan Lake their lifelong home. Employed as a cook and housekeeper for

Martha and Jack Flautt, she eventually became their caregiver too. Both of their wills showed how much they appreciated her.

On August 10, 2009, Sarah bade us farewell. I think of her with smiles and tears when I read a good novel. How she would have loved *The Help* and *Small, Great Things!*

*Nellie Ann and Sarah in their Sunday best in the late 1940s. Some women wore silk stockings during that time, but only a few could afford nylons, which were introduced at the 1939 World's Fair. Sarah and Nellie could afford neither silk nor nylons. But even in socks, they are chic ladies!*

Lurean, the seventh child, changed her name to Linda after she and her husband Welton Hawkins went their separate ways.

The mother of two girls and nine boys, Linda was forthright: if she thought you were good or bad, pretty or ugly, or anything in between, you heard it first from her.

How talented she was! A chef, dancer, designer, seamstress, comedian, raconteur, singer, choreographer, and so much more. There was no dance she couldn't do. If the current ones didn't meet her fancy, she simply created one to her liking. Oh my goodness! She had a way with all kinds of words, allowing no one to leave her presence without a laugh!

I hope she was smiling when she left us on September 9, 2010. When I remember her, my smile turns into outright laughter.

My parents had chosen the name Lorean for their tenth-born, but when the plantation owner's wife Ruth Flautt came to see the baby and made a fuss over her, oohing and aahing at how pretty she was and her beautiful head of hair, Mother made Ruth the first name.

Well, after seeing a movie starring Laraine Day, Ruth dropped her first name, changed her middle name to Lorraine, her preferred spelling, and never again answered to Ruth.

Adept at styling hair, Lorraine had a personality that lit up the room. And until she moved to Chicago around 1960—to live with Ethel—her feet gave Linda a run for the money on a dance floor.

Lorraine was the beloved mother of two daughters and three sons, devoted wife of Henry Jones, fun-loving aunt to many, and a protective sister to me. Trying to save me from my delusions, she said Nat King Cole would be too old to marry me by the time I became an adult. Ouch! All I could do was

"Pretend," and at the risk of sounding immodest, I did so almost as well as Nat sang.

Lorraine will always be known and loved for the joy she gave to others. How my heart ached when she went away on August 2, 1990. I miss her most at Christmastime.

*No pictures of us as children exist, if any were ever taken.*
*This one of me at twenty-two is less frightening than my earliest photo at fifteen.*

Unlike my siblings, I was a homely, scrawny, temperamental child—and such a tiny infant that Mother had to make a pillow for Sarah to hold and carry me safely.

In large families during dinosaur days, an older sibling often took care of a newborn because other youngsters needed the mother's attention. I was assigned to Sarah so that Mother could look after Lorraine and W C and take care of our house, as well as the Flautts'. Sarah proudly claimed me as her baby and catered to my every whim. Prone to crying spells and nose-bleeds, which Mother called "fits," I sobbed uncontrollably on Sarah's wedding day, begging her not to leave me. So, she and her husband took me to live with them for a few weeks. Angrier than thirteen red hornets when they brought me back home, I poured my heart out to the clouds, knowing Daddy understood.

Rosie Lee Powell Robinson, an alumna of Alcorn State University in Lorman, Mississippi, was wooed by John Buford Robinson until she said "I do." She and Jack—as he was known—became the parents of two girls and one boy.

Cousin Rose was not only a fashion maven, she was also a master teacher. One of the first Negro teachers assigned to a predominantly white school in Memphis, Tennessee, in the

1960s, she made our family proud, and her students too. To teach sixth-graders the proper use of objective and subjective pronouns, she sang "Take Me Out to the Ball Game." Then she explained, "Listen to how it sounds to say 'take *I* out to the ballgame,' or 'buy *I* some peanuts and cracker jacks,' or '*me* don't care if *me* never get back.'" The class roared, but they got it.

Was she ever a humorous storyteller! None of our relatives told family stories as well as she did. Losing her on February 22, 2014, was indeed painful. How I miss her and our late-night-to-early-morning phone conversations! Details about her role in my life are in the last chapter.

*My first employers, Jerome and Natalie Frager, became lifelong friends.*
*What a gracious and devoted pair—and real mensches too!*

On a road trip from Memphis to attend a Frager wedding in Kansas City, Jerry and Natalie took me with them to look after their three boys: ages six, five, and almost three. In 1961, they could eat at any restaurant along the way, but because of Jim

Crow laws, I could not: white-owned diners did not serve Negroes.

Mensch that he is, Jerry had Natalie, the boys, and me wait in the car when we stopped for lunch. To avoid the indignity of being told not to bring me into the restaurant, he had to tell the manager that I, his colored babysitter, would be joining him and his family, unless there was an objection, in which case he would go to another diner. In a few minutes, Jerry came back to the car and escorted Natalie, the boys, and me inside. I should also note that, as was customary at the time, I addressed Jerry and Natalie as Mr. and Mrs. Frager. More about their supporting role in the last chapter too.

*I was born in a house that looked almost exactly like this one, which is raised to keep snakes from slithering onto the porch and coming inside.*

Gazing at what remained of our second home in 1988, Mother appears to be lost in thoughts she never expressed. Respectfully, I think along with reminiscing, she is thanking the Lord for bringing her "such a mighty long way." A bit of hidden history about this house is in the next chapter, "She Kept Us Together."

*Our White Brick House*

Mother is standing on the north side of Second Dirt Road, a fictitious name used to facilitate this discussion. None of the roads had names when we lived in Swan Lake. When giving directions, we used ordinal numbers for roads and landmarks such as trees. To come to our house, visitors were told to turn right at the second dirt road and continue to the second white brick house.

The houses had neither numbers nor mailboxes. Mail was delivered to our box at the post office housed in the Flautts' general store. Today, the dirt roads are still nameless, but the main road on the west side of the plantation is now known as Flautt Road.

The west-to-east view in this photo is the last section of Second Dirt Road. Beyond the left side of the picture lay a huge pasture. Three of the four houses that comprised my neighborhood were at the pasture's southern edge. I was born in this pasture—well, not actually *in* the pasture—but in the second house on this road, a few yards to Mother's left.

*Second Dirt Road*

The plantation's cook lived up the road in a shotgun house that sat farther back in the pasture. Another brick house with a lovely little creek behind it was at the corner of Second Dirt Road and the main north-to-south gravel road on the east side of the plantation, which for this discussion will be called Flautt Road East.

Cows grazed in the pasture, and like in the picture of the white brick house, there were no fences around our homes. In the afternoon, a cow would usually come to our back door and moo until one of my siblings would go outside and milk her.

The stalks behind the fence on the right side of the road are cotton. In the spring, the entire field was covered with leafy, green stalks laden with buds that burst into white, yellow, and pink blossoms atop green bulbs pregnant with cotton. I imagined the section in front of our house as my rose garden.

The curve at the eastern end of the road leads to the Flautts' estate.

Whoa! I just realized our neighborhood was integrated, and we were the majority: one white family and nine Negro tenant farmers! Swan Lake's population included the three Flautt families and approximately eighteen Negro families, all tenant farmers.

Cotton was the major crop on our side of the main road; corn and bean fields were on the other side of Flautt Road East. The bean field ended at a south-to-north railroad that separated the plantation's eastern and western sections.

*Site of Our Last Home in Swan Lake*

A fire destroyed the house we lived in on this lot from December 1952 until December 1954. Starting at the front of the picture on the prior page, you are looking at our front yard, which abutted First Dirt Road on the south and Flautt Road East on the west, just beyond the front of this photo. To keep snakes away, the yards were bare when we lived in Swan Lake.

The corner of the large structure would have been a section of our front porch, and the small building in the background, a modern outhouse, sits on our side yard, where clotheslines were strung to hang our clothes to dry. Our heavy-duty washing machine, a large black kettle, sat in front of the big tree to the right of the outhouse. We washed our chenille bedspreads, sheets, and quilts in the kettle and our clothes in a tin tub, like the one hanging on the right side of the outhouse.

The tub did double duty as a portable bathtub. We would put a few buckets of cold water into it, bring at least two buckets of water to a boil on the kitchen stove, and pour the hot water into the tub. Rarely was the water at the right temperature, but at least we got a bath, the frequency of which shall remain a secret.

Our hen house was on the northeast side of the backyard, which would be on the left side of the photo, the back of our house. The garden was a few feet behind or north of the backyard, and the water pump, with the best water in the world, was in the middle of the yard. A small bean field was directly behind the garden, and the cotton field you saw in the photo of Second Dirt Road extended all the way south to the bean field.

The pigsty was on the right side of the garden, and our outhouse sat on the levee—an elevated ridge that protects crops from an overflow of a river during floods—a few feet above the pigsty. Trees in the background of this picture are along the bank of the Tallahatchie River, which is about a mile from the levee. A corn field sat in the space between the levee and the trees, and south of the corn field—which would be on the right side of the photo, a distance east of the big tree in the yard—lay a creek filled with the cutest minnows, some good-looking tadpoles, and a bunch of unattractive bullfrogs.

Our church was across the road, and the brick school was down the road from the church. In 1988, the school was used as a community center. Today, the building is vacant and in a state of disrepair.

Built without indoor plumbing in 1949, this was the first public school for Negro children in Swan Lake. Outhouses were constructed in an adjacent field, near the railroad track. I attended this school from third to sixth grade and I loved it, but not the lack of privacy at the privy: the outhouses did not have doors.

This juke joint was still standing in 1988. While I cannot describe its exact location, I know it was in an isolated field: anyone nearby would have been disturbed when the joint started jumping with harmonica blowing, guitar picking, fingers popping, and feet stamping.

After a week of chopping or picking cotton, men and women headed for the juke joint on Friday and Saturday nights. There, they "Let the Good Times Roll" at the "Saturday Night Fish Fry," feasting on fried catfish, coleslaw, slices of Wonder Bread, moonshine, and soda pops, along with peach cobbler for dessert in the summer, and pound cake in the winter.

Couples danced or listened to the blues. Some stayed long enough to close the place, but the churchgoers left around midnight. They had to catch a few winks before it was time to put on their Sunday best, go to church, and repent. Some religious people disapproved of dancing and listening to the blues, but not my family.

Sadly, the brick school, the Flautts' estate, and my memories are the only remaining relics of my Swan Lake life.

*The first school I attended in Memphis, and the most beautiful by far!*

*Bethlehem Baptist Church*
*I was baptized in this church, the first and only one we attended in Memphis.*
*Mother was an usher here just as she had been at her church home,*
*Bethlehem Missionary Baptist Church in Swan Lake.*

Dear Louise
i must say you
Railey ar giving
me my Flowers
while i am living
When i Past dont Crie
Just say i did my
Part for my Mother
i Pray and i ask
the good lord to
Bless you & family
and take Care of you When you ar Riding on
the streets

Sincere thanks
Is what
this brings,
But then, you
always
Do nice things!

*A Thank You Note from Mother*

A genteel lady, Mother always acknowledged favors and gifts with either a handwritten thank-you note or a printed one in which she added her own words of gratitude.

About two years before she passed, Mother called me and chuckled as she said, "I know I said you have given me flowers while I am alive, but I do want flowers on my grave." Not to disappoint her, I honored her wish, even banishing my tears when she died. During my visits to Memphis, weather permitting, I place fresh roses on her grave at Calvary Cemetery.

# She Kept Us Together ✍

*I* imagine my parents were in a state of anxiety at the beginning of 1943. The world was at war, and the United States was sending hundreds of thousands of soldiers to Great Britain and France. Undoubtedly, Daddy and Mother feared their eldest sons would be sent to Europe too. B was scheduled to report to Camp Shelby, Mississippi, for basic training on January 16; Fred had already completed his. I am sure Mother prayed for peace, her sons' safety, and comfort for mothers like herself. More than likely, Daddy prayed for the means to provide for his family without creating more debt than he could pay.

With only three of seven children old enough and strong enough to help him do more than plant seeds and pull weeds, Daddy worked from daybreak until nightfall. I believe fatigue and stress over money matters contributed to the tragic accident that ultimately took his life.

The following details about his mishap are based on answers to questions I asked as a child, along with bits and pieces of adult conversations I overheard.

By the crack of dawn, probably on the last Wednesday in July, Daddy had already sharpened some tools and started plowing the field he planned to finish before sundown. If he met his deadline, he would have time to water the horses—which he had to do every day—and repair a wagon. Working at a brisk pace, he plowed until a sharp pain in his right heel brought him to a quick stop. Lifting his foot, he saw the head of a nail in his brogans.

Daddy guided the mule to a tree, tied its reigns around the trunk, and took off the shoe, which pulled the nail out of his heel. Taking the sweat rag from around his neck, he pressed the wound to stop the bleeding. He then tightly wrapped his foot with the rag and waited a few minutes before putting on his shoe and going back to work. After plowing a few more rows, he took the mule to the barn and watered the horses, but left repairing the wagon for another day.

At sundown, Mother wondered why Daddy hadn't stopped by the house to take me with him to water the horses like he usually did. When he limped home with a makeshift bandage on his foot, she knew something terrible had happened. Daddy explained he had stepped on a rusty nail, but despite Mother's plea, he forbade her to ask Mr. Flautt to take him to the doctor. So she treated the wound herself.

Every day, while cleaning and re-dressing the wound, Mother pleaded with Daddy to go to the doctor, but he refused, continuing to work instead. But the day he came home complaining of being cold and asking for a quilt, Mother went to Mr. Flautt. Without hesitating, Mr. Flautt took Daddy to the hospital in Charleston, Mississippi, where he was diagnosed with sepsis: bacteria from the infected wound had entered Daddy's bloodstream.

Penicillin, which was brought to market in May 1942 and dubbed "the wonder drug," quickly became the antibiotic of choice for treating patients with sepsis. Although multiple companies—Glaxo, Merck, and Squibb, to name a few—were manufacturing the drug, they lacked enough plants to produce sufficient quantities for both the armed forces and civilians. With the country at war, priority was given to the military. Thus, civilian use was restricted to cases of treatment failure.[1]

To document that other therapies had failed, a doctor had to submit the patient's history with his request for penicillin. I do not know if this procedure was followed for Daddy or if doing so would have made a difference. Mother always said they arrived at the hospital too late. Daddy died on Sunday, August 8, 1943, at 5:30 p.m.

Left with seven children, ranging from fourteen months to fifteen years of age, Mother had very little money, and she could not find the cash Daddy had allegedly buried in the yard or hidden in the house. Her parents and siblings were deceased; she had only one aunt, maybe one or two cousins, and no nieces or nephews. Friends suggested she marry, and a few of Daddy's relatives asked her to give some of us to them.

Placing children who lost one or both parents with other relatives was a common and acceptable practice during dinosaur days—but not to Mother—and she had no intention of ever marrying again. To friends and relatives who offered such advice, she simply said, "No, thank you. No one can love my children like I do. I would be less than a mother to give even one of them away, and I will not put a stepfather over them. With the help of the good Lord, I will keep my children together and find a way to take care of them myself."

Mother remained on the Flautt Plantation, usually working as the housekeeper Thursday, Friday, and half the day on Saturday, and in the field with her older children Monday through Wednesday. Her income consisted of a small salary, $3 a day for chopping cotton, $1 for each one hundred pounds picked, and an annual settlement based on her share of the plantation's profits, less her balance at the general store. However, she did receive a monthly allotment for B's and Fred's service in the Army.

Unfortunately, B's service did not last long. The eldest son, he was torn between a desire to fill his unexpected role as head of our household and the obligation to serve our country. When he and Fred came home for Daddy's funeral, B would not have returned to Camp Shelby had Mother not ordered him to honor his word, the vow he took during his induction into the Army. But after a few weeks, B went A.W.O.L: absent without leave. He apparently found it too compromising to comply with the Army's disciplinary regulations while being subjected to its discriminatory practices.

It probably did not take long for the military police to find him because Camp Shelby is 228 miles south of Swan Lake, and B probably did not know anyone in the area. Having been taught to defend himself and to always stand up for what is right, B more than likely did not return without a fight. Soon, he was A.W.O.L. again—and again—until the Army turned his case over to the FBI.

Mother was surprised when the agents came to our home. She told them we had not seen B, but they did not take her word. From the stories I heard, Mother wasted no words in telling them B had just cause to desert: living in filthy barracks, being called ugly names, and having dirty tricks played on him with nothing being said or done. The agents ignored her, but they knew exactly what she meant; and after interrogating everyone, searching all around the house, and even peeking in the outhouse, they finally left.

Several days later, two agents found B sitting on a tractor in a field on another plantation, and they escorted him back to

Camp Shelby. This time, the commanding officer assigned B to a cell. While incarcerated, B wore the mask and kowtowed as expected. Sometime after his release, he snatched off the mask, grabbed his army knife, and made his way back to Swan Lake. No one ever came after him again. I consider B's desertion a one-man protest against the segregated military: he chose to desert with his dignity intact rather than to serve and have it degraded by discrimination.

With B back home, Mother probably felt more confident in her ability to keep us together. However, it seems she had barely adjusted to Daddy's death when kaboom! The love bug bit the three eldest of the seven children at home. During the second year of Daddy's passing, George married Ida Mae Green and moved to the King Plantation where her family lived. Then, moonstruck by love stories they read in *Modern Romance* and *True Confessions*, Sarah and Lurean jumped up and married too. Within four years, Lorraine and I were babysitting our new nieces and nephews.

In dinosaur days, parents taught their children how to do whatever chore they thought the child was big or old enough to do. At the ages of seven and five, Lorraine and I learned how to hold babies, feed and burp them, and change and wash their diapers too (there were no disposable diapers in dinosaur days). Sarah's daughter Mary was the first baby we took care of. With bright and dreamy eyes, a head full of soft curly hair, and chubby cheeks, she was the prettiest baby we had ever seen —but she cried a lot, or at least we thought she did.

One afternoon while I was holding Mary, she started to fuss. I rocked and cooed, but she continued nonetheless. I held her against my chest, with her head resting on my shoulder, and patted her back just as I had been told—and, you guessed it, still she cried. So I decided to put her back on my lap. As I was placing her head in a more comfortable position, she turned and her lip touched my hand. Before I could move it, she had latched onto my pinkie. I didn't know what to do, but since she had stopped crying, I just let her suck. Gradually, her eyes closed and she fell fast asleep. It would be Lorraine's turn to hold her when Mary woke up, and thinking by accident I had found a remedy for Mary's crying, I said, "If she cries, just put your finger in her mouth."

After spending the summer burping babies and changing diapers, Lorraine and I were more than ready for school, which began the first week in September and ended the second week in May. Mother appreciated education, but she needed the $2 per day J C and W C each earned. Consequently, their school year was only four to five months. They worked in the field during the summer, started school after crops were harvested in October or November, and left school around the first of March to plow the fields and plant new crops. Luckily, they learned to read and count well enough to avoid being cheated on payday.

By the spring of 1951, we were a family of fourteen, not including the critters who squatted near the pallet where Linda's daughter Kat and I slept. (Sarah and Linda probably came back home because their marriages were not like those they read about in magazines. But one of them would say this is none of my business.) One morning, right at the crack of dawn, I was awakened by a sharp pain in my pinkie, muffled squeaks, and movement against my cheek. I opened my eyes and saw a litter of tiny, pink, hairless mice snuggling right next to my face while their mother nibbled on my finger. I nearly knocked myself out slapping my face, and my wailing made the mother mouse abandon her babies. Just as I jumped into Mother's bed, I caught a glimpse of the rat's tail as she scuttled along the baseboard toward the back of the room.

While Mother tried to calm me down, Linda snatched Kat from the pallet. B burst into the room, and when he saw the orphaned mice—some still huddled where my head had lain and others floundering about looking for their mother—he quickly rolled the pallet over them, ran outside with it, and shook it to let the orphans fend for themselves.

The mice left an indelible mark on my psyche: I still cringe when anyone unexpectedly touches my face, especially the cheek, or stands too close to me. To avoid close contact with strangers, I will take multiple flights of stairs rather than ride a crowded elevator.

However, as often happens in traumatic incidents, something good came from this one.

Near the end of summer in 1953, Lorraine and I were playing in the front yard of the house on First Dirt Road when a white man in a pickup stopped to buy pecans. We didn't sell pecans, but a family up the road did. The man offered one of us a nickel to show him the way. I don't remember deciding to go with him, but I recall climbing into the cab.

As soon as we were out of Lorraine's sight, the man reached over, ran his hand up and down my cheek, and asked, "You wanna make some more money?"

Transported back to the incident with the mice, I jerked away and said a firm, "No, sir." Then I pressed myself against the door and leaned my head out the window.

After he bought the pecans, I jumped into the back of the truck and pretended not to hear him say, "Come on. Don't you want to ride inside?"

I rode back with him because I felt too dirty and ashamed to tell anyone what he had said and done, which I would have had to do if I had walked home. Besides, if Mother knew and did not get the sheriff before B found the man and made him disappear, B probably would have disappeared too, or even worse, become a piece of "Strange Fruit" on Swan Lake's hanging tree. Then we all would have suffered. With the stress of working six days a week and constantly adjusting her budget to keep us clothed and fed, Mother did not need any more heartaches.

If reading this makes you blue, you can imagine how depressing this time was for Mother. But she was a remarkably content and resourceful woman, and she never complained. When we outgrew our shoes, she cut off the back and made slides for us to wear in the summer. If we wore a hole in our shoes and part of the sole began to flop like it would come off, she would thread a big needle with a quadruple piece of thread and sew the sole back on, then she would put a piece of cardboard inside the shoe to cover the hole.

Regardless of her thrift, however, Mother had to charge items such as flour and material for our everyday clothes to her account at the Flautts' store. To avoid a surprise at settlement time, she spoke with Mr. Flautt about her debt. Whatever he said convinced her she could do better on the King Plantation.

After discussing the situation with B, Sarah, and Linda, Mother decided to move if the settlement was less than she needed to cover our expenses for the winter, without having to add more to her account at the store. Sure enough, after Mr. Flautt deducted her debt, the settlement was barely enough for the last few weeks of the year.

When Mother told Mr. Flautt we were moving, he asked her not to leave, emphasizing how much his family appreciated her, particularly his wife who didn't want anyone else to clean their house or especially to iron their clothes. (Mother was known for her scorch-less and wrinkle-free ironing.) Ever gracious, Mother explained that she had already spoken to Mr.

King, and her word was her bond. Billy and his wife Sarah (Mr. Flautt's younger son and daughter-in-law) told Mother if things didn't work out, she was always welcome to come back to Swan Lake and work for them. Kindly thanking them, Mother said, "I will certainly keep that in mind."

While packing to move, the whole family appeared to have the blues—instead of laughing, playing games, and telling jokes like we usually did at Christmastime, we were quiet and a bit grumpy. I felt like everything was wrong and not a thing would ever be right. Every landmark in our community was tugging at my heart: the wooden-frame house where I was born, the pasture, the two shotgun houses, the plantation owner's house, the walnut and pecan trees, the creeks and streams— not to mention Mr. Flautt's orchard and the three brick houses.

Oh my goodness! This reminiscing reminds me to tell the story about our white brick house. First some background information . . .

The United States became Great Britain's ally during World War II, a six-year conflict over Germany's expansion in Europe and Japan's in Southeast Asia. Consequently, when Britain captured more German soldiers than it had facilities to house, the United States transported several German POWs (prisoners of war) to a few of our military camps.

Two of the four camps located in Mississippi were less than fifty miles from Swan Lake, one about forty-one miles away, and the other near Clarksdale, just eighteen miles north of the Flautt Plantation.[2] With a shortage of labor from deploying so many young men to Europe, the United States allowed the Germans to work in various capacities. The proximity of the POWs to Swan Lake appears to support the story I heard about our white brick house.

According to oral family history, German soldiers built

our house and three more brick houses on the Flautt Planta-tion. Mother said the men wanted to install a commode in our house, but Mr. Flautt would not allow them to do so because he thought it would have been unfair to his tenants who lived in shotgun houses without plumbing. It seems living in a brick house was everybody's dream, and to add plumbing to ours would not only move us a notch above our Negro neighbors, it would also edge us a bit closer to the Flautts and perhaps be seen as favoritism. After all, Mother was their housekeeper.

But despite the house and our long history with the Flautts, Mother thought the time had come to make a change, which she hoped would be for the better.

## ♫ Accompaniments ♫

*I imagine after Daddy died, Mother would have been com-forted to hear Roberta Flack and Donny Hathaway's duet "Come Ye Disconsolate," and she would have been encour-aged by Aretha Franklin's solo, "The Lord Will Make a Way Somehow," which she so well knew. When she prayed for Fred's safety in Europe, many times she cried out, "Hear Me Lord." Although her plea lacked the African rhythms and guitar plucking that accompany Bonnie Raitt's plain-tive vocals, Mother's prayers were answered.*

*Fred and many thousand American soldiers came home safe and sound. How admirably those young men served our country! For example, the colored 332nd Fighter Group and the Japanese American 442nd Regimental Combat Team were among the most proficient of the 1.5 million Americans who fought in World War II. Because some whites believed Negroes lacked the ability to learn to fly, Jim Crow laws prevented colored men from training with white students. Consequently, men in the 332nd Fighter Group received their training at Tuskegee Institute, after which they overcame not only the bias of white pilots who refused to fly with them but also prejudice in the Air Force.*

*Despite the shortage of pilots, the Air Force rejected the world's first Negro pilot, Eugene Bullard (1895–1961). In his early teens, Bullard stowed away on a German ship to escape racism in Georgia. He made his way to France and joined the French Foreign Legion in 1914. After sustaining an injury that kept him from active duty, Bullard became a pilot and flew French bomber jets during World War I. Said to have been a fearless aviator, he flew twenty combat missions, shooting down a German aircraft on at least one. His derring-do earned him the moniker "Black Swallow of Death" in France.3*

*When finally given the chance to show their proficiency, the Tuskegee Airmen served as escorts for British and American bomber jets. I guess you could say that planes flying as escorts work like secret service agents: protecting bomber jets by flying above or beneath them to ensure they are not intercepted by enemy aircraft. The 332nd Fighter Group did not allow a single German plane to break through their escorts, and six of their planes sank a German destroyer—an unheard-of feat! The pilots—known as the "Red Tails" for their precision—destroyed over 300 enemy aircrafts. They received numerous medals, including at least eighty-five Distinguished Flying Crosses.4*

*Similarly, with a motto of "Go for Broke," the Japanese Americans in the 442nd Regimental Combat Team became the most highly decorated unit of World War II. Of the*

*14,000 men, 9,000 earned Purple Hearts. Twenty-one received Medals of Honor, and the unit received eight Presidential Unit Citations. No question, their first loyalty was to our country. Nonetheless, while the men volunteered to save American soldiers' lives in Europe, members of their own communities were involuntarily moved into internment camps here in America.*

*Japan's bombing of Pearl Harbor on December 7, 1941, caused some Americans to question the loyalty of Japanese Americans. To protect the United States from espionage and Japanese Americans from prejudiced whites, President Franklin D. Roosevelt signed Executive Order 9066 on February 19, 1942, mandating all persons of Japanese ancestry be relocated away from the western areas of Washington, Oregon, and California.5*

*Given only weeks to comply with the order, Japanese Americans did not have time to secure their properties or arrange for the management of their businesses, some of which were destroyed by looters and bigots by the time they were allowed to return. Both citizens and Japanese aliens were quickly moved to temporary relocation centers: fairgrounds and race tracks, surrounded by barbed wire, with converted livestock stalls as living quarters. Military police were on duty with guns mounted around the camps, pointed inward. When permanent facilities, known as internment camps, were built, the Japanese were again moved.*

*The camps were scattered among ten states as far inland as Arkansas. Lodgings were poorly constructed of fresh-cut wood that dried quickly and left gaps in the walls. Heated by wood stoves, the buildings had inadequate or no running water and only a communal latrine. Overcrowding, exposure to the elements, poor sanitation, malnutrition, and inadequate medical care caused or contributed to the deaths of many adults and children. Heart Mountain in Cody, Wyoming, was filled to capacity—10,000—for three years.*

*At least 117,000 Japanese Americans were interned on the mainland; only a few thousand were detained in Hawaii. Of the ten Americans convicted of spying for Japan during the war, not a single one was of Japanese ancestry. In the Civil Liberties Act of 1988, the United States apologized for the unjust relocation of Japanese Americans and authorized a $20,000 payment to those who had been placed in the camps.6*

*While the "Airmen," Japanese American soldiers, my brother Fred, and scores of Negro servicemen survived the military's racist tactics, six million European Jews lost their lives during the Holocaust, the result of Adolph Hitler's (1889–1945) attempt to create a pure or master race. Hitler is also responsible for the death of an additional four to six million people he considered undesirable: gypsies, anyone who was handicapped, the mentally ill, homosexuals, and those sympathetic to the Jews. It is speculated that Hitler committed suicide in prison; some of his accomplices were tried and convicted of crimes against both peace and humanity during the famous Nuremberg Trials held in Nuremberg, Germany (1945–1949).*

*In 1960, Israeli intelligence agents captured Adolf Eichmann (1906–1962), the logistical mastermind of the concentration camps, where Jews were subjected to some of the most inhumane treatments, including experiments, gassing, and starvation. The agents accomplished their incredible mission in nine days, arriving in Buenos Aires, Argentina, on May 11, 1960, and flying back to Israel on May 20, with Eichmann in tow. In Tel Aviv, Eichmann was tried and convicted on fifteen counts of crimes against humanity. He was hanged on June 1, 1962. The movie* Operation Finale *is a spellbinding depiction of his capture.*

*When the Holocaust ended in 1945, Tuskegee Institute was entering its thirteenth year as the site for the forty-year "Tuskegee Study of Untreated Syphilis in the Negro Male" (1932–1972). An experiment on 399 men with syphilis and 201 without the disease, the study replaced the Public Health Service's program of documenting and treating syphilis in the rural African American population.*

*Told they were being treated for "bad blood" and enticed with free transportation to hospitals, meals, medicine for other conditions, and burial insurance, the men—most of whom were illiterate sharecroppers—agreed to participate in the study. Like the title indicates, the doctors conducting the study did not treat any of the men for syphilis; however, some of them wrote and published articles about it in medical journals.*

*By the time an exposé of the experiment appeared in* The New York Times *on July 26, 1972, only seventy-four of the participants who had syphilis were alive. An investigation of the study found:*

- *There was no evidence the researchers had informed the men of the study or of its real purpose.*

- *The men had been misled, had not received the facts needed to give informed consent, and had not received adequate treatment for their disease.*

*In 1973, civil rights attorney Fred Gray (1930–) filed a class-action lawsuit on behalf of the study's participants and their families. The government agreed to a $10 million out-of-court settlement in 1974, which included lifetime medical benefits and burial services for all living participants in the study. In 1975, the United States added the same benefits for* *wives, widows, and offspring. On May 16, 1997, President Bill Clinton apologized to five survivors and the families of the victims of the Tuskegee Study. The last participant died in 2004.*

*Like the internment camps, the Tuskegee Study is an unsightly chapter in our country's history, a chapter that created distrust of the medical community and governmental agencies among some African Americans. Yet, we persevere in our efforts to make unalienable rights a living reality for everyone in our battered and blemished, but beloved "America the Beautiful," soulfully saluted by Ray Charles. And also by the godfather of soul, James Brown, in "Living in America."*

# Hope for Greener Pastures

The wind didn't blow, the sun didn't shine, and the sky hid behind a thick blanket of clouds all day long. Such was the day we moved to the King Plantation.

With our possessions crammed into a wagon hitched to a pickup, we went north on Flautt Road East and turned right at the border of the King and Flautt Plantations. As the truck crept around the bend, I noticed a dramatic contrast in the landscape.

Except for a few barren stalks in a lonely cotton field, the right side of the road looked rather benign, but the left side was absolutely eerie. Greenish-gray moss hung from cypress trees, dense vines wrapped themselves around pine and birch branches, weeds and clumps of wild grass covered the ground. Hidden behind all that vegetation lay a swamp known to swallow men alive. I tell you, the thought of living by a swamp with trees pushing and shoving each other was scary enough, but when Mother said some of the vines were poison ivy, my entire body twitched. What a relief when we turned onto a dirt road!

Looking toward the end of the road and seeing a house, I began to feel hopeful. But the closer we got, the less hopeful I felt. By the time we arrived, I felt completely helpless as well as hopeless. Made of cracked weather-worn wood, and surrounded by cotton, corn, and bean fields, the house was close to being in the middle of nowhere. Not a single neighbor's home was in sight! A majestic black walnut tree posing in the left corner of the back yard, its branches suspended over a modest chicken coop, was the only hint of landscaping.

Inside, a fireplace gave atmosphere to the front room—the only one with electricity. But the house was barely adequate for our family of eleven: Mother assigned the front room, which did double duty as a family room, to B and his wife Jeanette; she gave the larger of two bedrooms to J C, W C, Lorraine, and me; and she kept the smaller one for herself, Sarah, and her three toddlers. A potbelly heater kept the room I shared with my siblings warm.

Cramped in an isolated house during the longest, leanest, and coldest winter of my life, I did my best to behave—that is, until I had a run-in with Jeanette.

On a Saturday afternoon, around the end of January, Jeanette stormed into the bedroom that J C, W C, Lorraine, and I shared just as I was stepping out of our portable bathtub. Eyes glaring and nose flaring, she grabbed me by my left shoulder and said, "Why did you lie on me and tell Willie I had a man?"

Wondering what she meant, I simply stared at her. In a flash, Jeanette either loosened her grip or pushed me. I felt myself falling, face first, straight toward the potbelly heater. Turning to protect my face, I reached for a large nail in the wall. The moment I wrapped my hand around the nail, I heard a sizzle. "Aaah!" I cried out. The outside of my left leg had struck the heater. Jerking it away left a strip of skin about five inches long and two inches wide on the heater and a ghastly wound in my leg. When I saw the pinkish-yellow gash, with every nerve and blood vessel exposed, I screamed at Jeanette, "Look at what you did!"

Mother heard the ruckus and came into the room. I told her what Jeanette had said and that she had pushed me. Jeanette denied it. Surely, she didn't intend to push me toward the heater, but if she hadn't come into the room, the accident wouldn't have happened. Mother knew only one of us was telling the truth, but she loved her daughter-in-law as much as she loved me. Instead of chastising Jeanette, she called for Sarah to bring the home remedy kit. Despite being cash-strapped, as soon as she patched up my leg, Mother took me to the emergency room.

The hospital visit left only enough money to prepare two meals a day for the next four months. Breakfast was biscuits and molasses or hoecakes and molasses, with sweet milk or buttermilk. Dinner was more varied: either collard, mustard, or turnip greens, or beans with cornbread and a baked yam; or buttermilk, cornbread and baked sweet potatoes, or a sandwich of candied yams and biscuits, or black-eyed peas and corn-bread; or one of my favorites: turnip bottoms and rutabagas seasoned with pepper, onions, and salt pork. Regardless of what was served, after eating dinner in the afternoon and having no supper in the evening, we all went to bed hungry.

Mother coped with our situation by praying and reading her Bible. Every morning we were awakened by the sound of her voice as she prayed:

> Our Father who art in Heaven, thank you for waking me up this morning, being clothed and in my right mind. I ask you to bless my children. Enable me to work and provide for them. I know they are hungry

and must be fed. They need clothes. Please, Father, help me to see my way clear to get the clothes they need and food to feed them. I know you are a God of mercy and justice. I know you stand up for the righteous and widows. You said you would be a mother for the motherless and a father for the fatherless. I know you can make a way out of no way. I put my entire faith and trust in you and ask you to please hear my prayer. Please protect my children. Do not let any evil or harm come to them. Lord, I ask you to comfort the sick and the afflicted. Heal all those who are suffering and in pain; keep me from all hurt, harm, and danger. In the name of Jesus I pray. Amen.

This is a condensed version of her prayer—she prayed about everything and for everyone—which she spoke in a cadence that varied with each sentence. I often wondered how much longer she would pray. Not an early riser, I wanted Mother to hurry and finish so I could go back to sleep. I didn't know her prayers were a blessing I desperately needed.

Instead of praying, I stayed in my place—not speaking until spoken to, except for imaginary conversations with Daddy. How anxious I was for the wound to heal! And when it finally did, instead of turning my socks to just above the ankle, as was fashionable, I left them up to partially cover the unsightly scar on my leg. (Girls and ladies usually did not wear pants in dinosaur days.)

In addition to talking to Daddy, I visualized myself living in a mansion with a rose garden in the backyard, a cupboard filled with enough dried fruits and canned goods to last forever, and a chifforobe of pretty outfits like the ones in Alden and Spiegel's catalogs. (Most homes, including ours, didn't have closets: instead, we placed our clothes in a large piece of furniture called a chifforobe.)

Mother's prayers during that difficult winter inspired Lorraine and me to do more to help her. One day, after everyone went to a field on the other side of the plantation, we decided to chop the cotton in the field across the road from our house. We chopped almost two rows, but the pride we had in our misguided good deed didn't last long.

Horrified when she saw what we had done, Mother exclaimed, "That field was not ready to be chopped! How am I ever going to explain what y'all did to this man's cotton?"

Well, the answer was making us replant the seedlings, most of which were bent and bruised. Mother, bless her heart, even helped us.

Instead of trying to chop cotton again, Lorraine and I paid more attention to our job of babysitting. Actually, she babysat while I sat beside the radio listening to baseball games.

Having seen how quickly I learned the timetables, my brothers knew I had a good memory, so they asked me to listen to the games for them. Certain they would pay to hear how Roy Campanella, Don Newcombe, Pee Wee Reese, Joe DiMaggio, and their all-time favorite Jackie Robinson played— if he stole a base, hit a home run, threw or tagged anyone out, or caught a fly ball—I said, "I'll remember the whole game, for a nickel."

Acting bossy, J C said, "Okay, but if you mess up, you ain't getting nothing."

He knew I wasn't going to "mess up."

"Okay," W C agreed with a smile. What a sweet boy he was!

Not only did I memorize the game, but also the players on each team and the announcers. Imitating either Vin Scully, Dizzy Dean, Curt Gowdy, or Red Barber, I gave my brothers a play-by-play report on each inning. And like Mother told us to do, I saved some of my nickels.

By October 1952, Mother's hope for greener pastures on the King Plantation had faded. Land that had looked fertile failed to produce large crops, which meant our settlement would not be, as she put it, "nearly enough for us to make a living there." So she decided to return to Swan Lake and work for Billy and Sarah Flautt. Now that was the best news I had heard all year long, but before I could "Jump Up and Shout," Mother dropped the bomb: we would not live in our old neighborhood on Second Dirt Road because another lady had already moved into the white brick house that had always been ours. Seeing me about to pitch a fit, Mother said we would be closer to school in our new home, then she gave me a sermon, telling me it wouldn't be right to have Mr. Flautt ask the woman to move. Like Nat King Cole's "Mona Lisa," I just smiled to hide my broken heart. And between the two of us, I believed Nat was actually singing to me.

♫ *Accompaniments* ♫

℗

*A year on the King Plantation was enough for us to know the truth in Etta James's "The Blues Don't Care." And Joe Williams must have heard B thinking, "Every Day I Have the Blues." But Mother didn't need the Staple Singers to tell her to "Pray on My Child." She began and ended each day in prayer. Oh, "If I Could Hear My Mother Pray Again," I would gladly listen as long as she prayed! In the meantime, Mahalia Jackson's vocals will have to do.*

# Eight Dollars
## and Five Cents

From the King Plantation, we traveled south on Flautt Road East, passed our old neighborhood on Second Dirt Road, and stopped at a lone wooden-frame house located on the north side of First Dirt Road about a mile west of the Tallahatchie River. With a large front room, two bedrooms, and a nice-size kitchen, the house was the largest one we had ever lived in. The design, location, and size compensated for the loss of our brick house.

J C liked being near the river because Mr. Flautt had given him a job of measuring the water levels, which was a means of predicting floods and droughts. Unlike the rest of us, he was not afraid of the rickety wooden bridge spanning the river. The bridge rattled and shook when anything with wheels approached, and the boards squeaked when we walked on it. Two horizontal iron rods on each side of the bridge served as guardrails, but there was no netting to prevent us from falling into the muddy water. None of this, however, mattered to J C.

Promoting himself as the weatherman, J C bragged about never making a mistake when he leaned over the rails and lowered the measuring device to the bottom of the river at dawn, noon, and sunset. Obviously, J C's work was satisfactory because Mr. Flautt gave him a second job: releasing insecticide over the cotton fields from the crop duster airplane to prevent the boll weevil from destroying the plants.

Well, by the time J C finished telling Mother about the job, she had "put on the mask," which she rarely wore, and was on her way to have a talk with Mr. Flautt. She asked him to please explain why he had offered her child such a dangerous job without speaking to her first. To allay her fears, Mr. Flautt described how J C would be positioned and securely strapped in the plane, with all precautions taken to ensure his safety.

Although J C was four months shy of eighteen, he was still a minor. No way would Mother have Mr. Flautt view her as an irresponsible parent, or ignorant of her rights. However, besides needing the extra money J C would make, Mother knew he was capable of doing the job, so she accepted the explanation as an apology, confirmed the salary, and gave her consent.

In addition to promoting himself as a weatherman, J C started boasting about being a pilot. With his bravado and driving skills, I have no doubt he could have been a pilot—or even a race car driver. Once, I saw a train behind us when he was driving W C, Lorraine, and me to Nellie's house. A few yards before we reached the curve near Second Dirt Road, I looked over at him and said, "J, can you beat the train to Nellie Ann's?" (Sometimes, we called him J.)

"Sure, I can," he chuckled.

He shifted into high gear, floored the accelerator, and sped around the curve like Mario Andretti. With one eye on the train and the other on the road, I cheered, "Go, J C, go! Faster! Faster! Don't let him catch you!"

J C probably got to Nellie's faster than Andretti could have. He and I were so mischievous. Mother never knew what he would do or what I would say. When she lined us up to whip us, I would try to negotiate; but J C would either grab the switch, climb a tree, or attempt to run away, only to be caught and given extra licks. Corporal punishment was Mother's discipline of choice for disobedience, such as helping ourselves at the Flautts' orchard, which she had told us never to go near. She reserved tongue lashings for rudeness and for adults who made the wrong move, like Mr. Flautt did on J C's first payday.

When J C came home with a small piece of change that was nowhere near what one would have made flying an airplane, Mother thought he had spent some of his pay. But J C insisted Mr. Flautt had paid him the right amount. Reaching for her sunhat, Mother exclaimed, "Oh, no! He owes you more."

Tying the bonnet, she stormed out of the house, straight to the general store. As soon as she opened the door, Mr. Flautt looked like he knew trouble had arrived. Mother recognized the look, but she addressed him respectfully anyway. "Mr. Flautt, may I have a word with you, please, sir?"

She reminded him of the additional money he owed J C, but Mr. Flautt said he had paid enough because J C was a boy.

Hands on her hips, Mother replied, "If he was man enough to do the job, he is man enough for you to pay him what you said you would. Now you mean to tell me you ain't going to honor your word?"

Smiling as he turned away from her, Mr. Flautt said, "Go on home now, Lula."

Not to be outdone, Mother proclaimed, "This ain't over with yet."

Instead of walking back to our house, she stepped across the railroad track, turned right, and headed north on Flautt Road West, straight to Sumner, nine miles away. She was going to report Mr. Flautt to "the law," who she hoped would order him to pay the rest of J C's salary.

Standing within earshot of the conversation, Mr. Flautt's son, Jack, decided to go after Mother. They both knew that receiving justice from "the law" was highly unlikely for her. (Calling a sheriff "the law" may have been the Negroes' way of reminding him of his responsibility.)

Fully aware of her rights, Mother knew any chance for justice on earth began with reporting misdeeds to the proper authorities. Furthermore, she was doing what she always told us: "If you lay down, people will walk all over you, step on you, and stomp you too. Always stand up for yourself and for what is right, tell the truth, use your head, and don't let nobody outsmart you."

As for Jack, although he may have intervened to prevent Mother from filing a report that could have tarnished his family's reputation, he always treated us with respect. When he caught up with her, Jack steered the truck to the edge of the road and called out, "Lula, it's too far for you to walk to Sumner, and you don't need to. Come on now, get in the truck so I can take you home." (Because of Jim Crow's lingering effect, I admit to feeling a bit out of sorts for not referring to him as "Mr. Jack" like I always did.)

Looking straight ahead, Mother said, "I'm not going home 'til I get the law to make you pay what you owe J C."

With her confident stride, she kept right on walking. Everyone recognized Mother's walk. Shy of five feet, with a healthy quadruple-D chest, she took power steps. When they felt vibrations only her size-six feet could make, every rock and clump of dirt that wanted to remain in one piece scampered to the other side of the road.

Forced to accept that Mother meant what she said, Jack put the money in his hand, held it up so she could see the dollar bills, and said, "All right, Lula, here's the rest of the money. Now, come on, let me take you home."

Glad to see that Mr. Flautt had honored his word, Mother thanked Jack as she accepted the bills and his offer of a ride. (I say Mr. Flautt because that is the only name we ever used for him.)

Although she now had enough money to buy material for Sarah and Linda to make our school clothes and to buy our shoes, Mother had to make a decision about my schooling. Because of Daddy's parting words to take care of me and her concern about my health, Mother had allowed me to repeat the fourth grade. But concerned that I would fall too far behind, she had strong reservations about permitting me to spend yet a third year with my teacher Mrs. Dora Carr. As for me, I would have been content to stay. Like my sister Ethel, Mrs. Carr was neat and well-groomed, which I favored. The fifth-grade teacher, on the other hand, was not quite as tidy.

Obsessed with cleanliness, I was horrified to witness this teacher blow her nose several times on the same handkerchief—I thought she should have gotten a clean hankie. Unable to imagine her touching my lessons or me with germs on her hands, I was adamant about not being a student in her classroom.

The summer before I was to become one of the bacteria-exposed fifth-graders, we went to town to see a movie. A horror film of the worst kind, *The Iron Claw,* was showing. From the moment I first saw the claw until "The End" came on the screen, I clung to Lorraine in fear.

As soon as we got home, I rushed to bed and pulled the covers over my head, trying to hide from the horrible images of the black iron claw. Well, that didn't work. I had the worst nightmares, felt cold all over, and hardly slept a wink. Barely able to get out of bed, I couldn't eat breakfast on Sunday, and I was too nervous to go to church. I had another fitful night and remained in bed almost all day on Monday. When Mother came home and saw I was still in bed, she said, "You don't look right. I'm taking you to the doctor tomorrow."

On Tuesday morning, we went to a doctor in Glendora, the closest town with a medical office. After Mother described my symptoms, he gave me a thorough examination, listening to my heart over and over again. Finally, he had heard enough to make his diagnosis: a "weak heart," which he said meant Mother should keep me away from anything that might be frightening, overtaxing, or upsetting. (The term "weak heart" is not medically correct; the doctor merely used it to explain that he had heard something unusual, but not serious. Yet, even today, I avoid films with disturbing or scary subjects.) You can imagine how thrilled I was when Mother decided to allow me to repeat the fourth grade, rather than risk overtaxing my weak heart by forcing me into the fifth-grade teacher's classroom. But when school started in 1953, she had an abrupt change of heart. So, into the germ zone I went.

Of all my teachers, the fifth-grade teacher is the only one whose name I do not remember. What I do recall about fifth grade is becoming proficient in language arts and fractions and daydreaming about how cute some of the dresses in Sears & Roebuck, Spiegel, and Alden catalogues would make me look.

Convinced two dresses in Alden's 1953 spring catalog were made for me, I showed them to Mother, but she could order only one. Well, I had to have both, so I convinced her to let me pick cotton. Then, before the World Series began, I raised my fee for listening to the games from a nickel per regular-season game to a quarter per play-off and World Series game. I picked cotton two or three times, saving what I earned each time and adding it to my baseball earnings.

J C and W C knew I was saving my money, and when they

had spent all of theirs, they would ask me for a loan. Short on money to order the dresses, I put my math skills to work and found that charging them twenty-five cents for each quarter they borrowed would make up the shortage with a few cents left. Knowing how cunning I was and wanting money to buy candy bars, marbles, snow cones, and soda pops, they agreed to the terms.

Between my savings, loan repayments, and baseball salary, I was finally able to order the dresses. You can imagine my excitement when they arrived! One was navy blue with a white sailor's collar. The other was striped: turquoise, yellow, and white horizontal stripes on the bodice, with the same colors and diagonal stripes in the skirt. This dress had a lovely, round white collar and a belt. I wore those dresses with pride, and I was glad to have done something to help Mother—because to everyone's dismay, we did not get a settlement in November.

Now, to the best of my memory, not only had J C been a weatherman and a pilot, he had also worked in the field with the rest of the family. In addition to field work, Mother had babysat, ironed, and cleaned house for Billy and Sarah Flautt. She had not bought much on credit and was looking forward to a nice settlement. However, in late November, she discovered the settlement was not enough to cover her debt at the general store. Clearly, it was time to leave Swan Lake for good, but Mother would not leave owing anybody. So she decided not to buy anything else on credit, even if it meant rationing food again.

BY THE SPRING of 1954, we were a family of eight: Sarah, two of her children, Mother, J C, W C, Lorraine, and me. Occasionally, Mother had to buy flour and meal on credit at the general store, but she paid something on her debt each payday. With everyone—except me—working in the field, she expected the settlement that coming winter would be large enough to cover her balance at the store, and for us to move too.

In August, Fred and Alice came to our annual family picnic with their three-month-old baby Marino who seemed to like me quite a lot. Seeing how Marino and I took to each other, Fred asked Mother if he could take me to Memphis for a while. To avoid one of my fits and taxing my weak heart, Mother said, "Yes, but only for two weeks because she has to start school next month." In no time at all, I had carefully packed my clothes and was ready to hit the road in Fred's new car.

When we turned off Flautt Road West onto Highway 49, I asked Fred if he could make the telephone poles spin. He knew exactly what I meant and said, "Okay. Let me see what this car can do."

In no time at all, his green-and-white Buick had the poles whirling, and they didn't stop until we reached the Tennessee state line. All along the way, Alice whispered, "Slow down now. You don't have to drive so fast."

She may have been scared, but I certainly wasn't. Everyone in our family knew Fred was the best driver in Mississippi. I loved hearing Mother tell the story of how he handled the car when oncoming traffic forced him to veer toward the shoulder. She said, "We were headed straight into a ditch along the side of the highway, but Fred held on to that steering wheel, turning it one which a-way and then another until we got back on the road."

Although nothing that exciting happened on the way to Memphis, I enjoyed the ride, and my stay was close to the life in my dreams. Little did I know my dream of living in the city would become a reality before the year ended.

AT SETTLEMENT TIME, Mother thought there must be a mistake. Having planted, chopped, and picked more cotton; pulled and shucked more corn; and picked more beans than ever before, she was expecting a lot more than $8.05. But Mr. Flautt assured her there was no mistake. Mother thought of telling him he ought to be ashamed of himself, but she appealed to him as a parent instead. Looking him straight in the eye, she said, "As a father, you surely can understand how I feel seeing my children go to bed hungry almost every night, taking them to work in the field instead of sending them to school, and watching them wear clothes and shoes they have outgrown. They deserve better, and it's up to me to see they have food and live where they can get an education and make something of themselves. Since they don't have that opportunity here, I have decided to move to Memphis." Sensing his empathy, she then asked if he would be so kind as to ask Sarah Flautt to write a letter of recommendation for her. He assured her that he would.

Recalling that a lack of money had kept her from continuing her education, Sarah gave Mother $5 toward school expenses for W C, Lorraine, and me. With all our belongings packed in the trunk of Fred's Buick and only $13.05 in cash, Mother was grateful for the opportunity to start anew in Memphis.

Shortly after passing the Tennessee state line, Fred turned off Highway 61 and made a left turn onto South Parkway. He continued to Kansas Street, made another left until he reached Silver Age, then turned right. At the end of Silver Age, Fred made a U-turn and parked in front of what I considered an upscale apartment complex.

Ten gray-and-white single-story clapboard buildings filled

the entire south side of the street, the prettiest block on Silver Age. A wide, grassy median divided the complex down the middle. A sidewalk and three buildings perpendicular to the street were on each side of the median; the two buildings at the southern end of the complex were parallel to Silver Age. Each building had two two-bedroom apartments, front and back doors, front yards, and a walkway to a front porch.

Fred's apartment was the second one in the first perpendicular building on the west side of the complex. While he, Mother, W C, and Lorraine unloaded the car, I followed Alice into the house, where I had to be careful not to slip and fall. The waxed floor glistened like a sheet of ice, and every piece of furniture looked like an expensive, untouchable antique.

Impressed, but not overwhelmed, Mother looked at Alice and Fred and said, "The Lord has blessed you. You certainly do have a nice home. Now, please don't think I don't appreciate your letting us stay here, but as soon as I find work, I'll look for a place for my children and me."

Mother understood that relatives helped each other: whoever had the most was expected to reach out to those in need. But she also knew that Fred and Alice needed time to themselves. They had been married only two years, their first child was seven months old, and their second was expected in five months. Respectful of their home, Mother told us not to touch or do anything in the apartment without Alice's permission.

For the first time in our lives, we had indoor plumbing, electric lights in every room, a refrigerator, and a gas stove, not to mention a TV and a telephone. Alice taught us how to make a call on the two-party telephone line she and Fred shared with another family. In dinosaur days, telephone conversations were transmitted over wires, called lines. Based on what they could afford, families had a single line or shared a two-party or even a three- or four-party line. Alice told us if we picked up the receiver and heard someone talking, the other family was using the line and we should put the receiver back in the cradle and wait until the line was clear. Knowing no one in Memphis, we did not need to use the phone. However, curiosity often got the best of all of us—except Mother and Fred.

Finding a church was far more important to Mother than using a phone, and she joined the first one she saw: Bethlehem Baptist Church on Ingle Avenue. Having been an usher at her church in Swan Lake, Mother explained that as a widow with three children, she could not serve on Bethlehem's Usher Board until after she had found a job and was settled in her own home. Touched by her testimony, the minister asked the congregation to give Mother a monetary welcome, for which she was most grateful. But when she came home with her good fortune, Fred—proud man that he was—urged her not to tell our business to strangers. Mother saw the congregation as her "church family" and told him, "It's better to be humble enough to ask for bread and eat than to be too proud to ask and starve."

Considering our situation, as well as his age and grade level from having spent more time in the field than in the classroom, W C decided to work instead of attend school. Reluctantly, Mother agreed he would work until the two of them had saved enough money for our own place, after which he would finish his schooling.

To find work, Alice explained they would have to take a streetcar to the employment office in downtown Memphis.

"Now," she cautioned them, "after you get on the streetcar and pay your fare, go all the way to the back of the bus. You may have to move if you sit near the front."

Memphis had strict segregation laws, one of which reserved the front seats in all public transportation for whites.

After paying their fares, Negroes had to take seats in the rear, beginning with the last row. If all the front seats were taken when other white passengers boarded the bus, Negroes seated in the first rows behind the white section gave their seats to the White passengers and moved to the rear. Oh, the irrationality of racism! I would much rather find an empty seat anywhere on the bus than sit in one still steaming from anybody's heat.

In mid-December, Mother took the bus to the employment office, arriving a few minutes before it opened. Shortly after her arrival, a clerk opened the door, gave a slip of paper with a number on it to each person in line, and told everyone to take a seat and wait until her number was called. When Mother's number was called, she went to the desk of a Mrs. Matthews.

"Do you have any experience?" Mrs. Matthews asked.

"Yes, ma'am," my mother said politely.

Mrs. Matthews nodded. "Do you want daywork?"

Taking Sarah Flautt's recommendation from her purse, Mother said, "Yes, ma'am, this letter vouches for me, and I will take whatever work you have."

Mrs. Matthews read the letter, excused herself, and went to another representative's desk. Mother overheard her say to the lady, "Have you ever seen such a beautiful letter of recommendation? We won't have any trouble finding work for this girl." (Calling Mother a "girl" was another lingering effect of slavery.)

She then came back to her desk and said, "I'm going to find work for you today. Now, I may not be able to get you a full-time job, but if you'll take days, I can get that for you. With your reference, anyone would be glad to have you work for them. Just have a seat over there until I call you."

Having waited patiently for some time, Mother was nodding off when she heard "Lula Blocker." She abruptly raised her head. "Yes ma'am," she said and walked over to Mrs. Matthews's desk. (Saying "Yes, ma'am" to a woman half her age was yet another lingering effect.)

"I have a job for you—two days a week. The pay is three dollars a day, and car fare."

"Oh, thank you, Jesus!" Mother said.

"When can you start?" Mrs. Matthews asked.

Smiling faintly, Mother answered, "I can start today."

"Well," Mrs. Matthews said, seeming to think it over, "how about you start the day after next? I'd like you to stay put while I look for more days."

Mother agreed, but as work orders were slow that time of year, Mrs. Matthews did not find more work.

"I'll continue to look," she promised.

Mother thanked Mrs. Matthews and agreed to come to the office until she had five days of work.

I should note here that a dayworker was a lady who cleaned houses by the day because the women who hired her either could not afford a full-time maid or did not have enough work for five days a week. It seems daywork was the only part-time position available for many Negro women who did not need or want to work full-time or for those who were not trained in a profession such as cosmetology, nursing, or teaching and for colored women who could not find employment as elevator operators or ladies' room attendants in department stores, or housekeepers at hotels. Clerical positions were available only with companies owned by Negroes.

While we were ecstatic over Mother's good news, she expressed her gratitude humbly through prayer. That night, kneeling beside her pallet in the living room, she thanked the Lord for enabling her to find work and to see another Christmas in a better place. She reminded Him that He said He would be a father to the fatherless, a mother to the motherless and a friend to widows. She asked Him to bless each of us, especially Fred and Alice, their baby Marino, the one on the way, and all of her children and loved ones in Swan Lake.

Things were certainly looking up, and as 1954 came to a close, I was eager for January to arrive when I would enroll in my new school: Riverview Elementary.

## ♫ Accompaniments ♫

*How glad I was that Mother listened to the voice, saying, "You've Got to Move." I think Lorraine wanted to shout "Amen." Lou Rawls's rendition of these songs is one of the best. As for W C and me, we were glad to leave Huddie Leadbelly's "Cotton Fields." Better known as Lead Belly, he was possibly the most prolific composer of blues, gospel, and folksongs during his time (1888–1949). But, unlike John Denver (1943–1997), we had had our fill of "Country Roads" that took us to the movies in Webb.*

*Although the films depicted Native Americans as the bad guys and the white settlers who were confiscating the tribes' land as the good ones, westerns were our favorite. Like our textbooks, none of the "cowboy movies"—as we called them— included colored cowboys, Negro families who settled in the West, or the "Buffalo Soldiers," Negro infantrymen who intervened in clashes between Native Americans and white settlers whose migration fulfilled the United States's "manifest destiny." Native Americans called the men buffalo soldiers because they fought so bravely.[1] But not all the soldiers were men.*

*When her slaveholder's farm was seized in Jefferson City, Missouri, Cathay Williams (1842–1892?) was forced to accompany the 8th Indiana, a Union regiment, in December 1861. She served as the officers' novice cook until demoted to laundress. In 1866, she assumed a male persona, joined the Army, and became a Buffalo Soldier under the pseudonym William Cathey. After almost two years of soldiering, Williams tired of army life. She feigned an illness, her gender was discovered, and she was discharged from the Army on October 14, 1868. Williams resumed her female identity and had a short-lived marriage. Self-employed as a cook, seamstress, and laundress, she died in Trinidad, Colorado.*

*How I would have enjoyed movies about the Buffalo Soldiers and African cowboys and cowgirls such as Nat Love (1854–1921) and Mary Fields (1832–1914)!*

*Known as "Deadwood Dick," Nat Love left Tennessee in 1869 to live a life filled with adventure, including being adopted by a Native American tribe, riding a hundred miles on an unsaddled horse for twelve hours, and surviving over fourteen bullet wounds. At least that is the story he is said to have told in his autobiography, which was written in 1907.[2]*

*Standing six feet tall and the fastest to hitch a team of six horses, Mary Fields became the first African American woman to work for the United States Postal Service. Almost sixty when she was hired, Fields delivered mail over hills, through valleys, and in rain, sleet, and snow. Her reliability and handling of the coach earned her the moniker Stagecoach Mary.*

*Yes, movies about Negro frontiersmen and women—more than this book can hold—would not only have been entertaining and educational, they also might have kept us from being duped into accepting "our place": we entered the movie theater from a side door and sat in the rear or in the balcony. After the movie, Lorraine and I would buy a malt or milkshake at the drugstore next to the theater. Unlike white children who could sit at the counter and enjoy their beverages, we had to stand, place our order, and drink ours outside. Once, I tried to sit on a stool, but the owner shook his head and said, "Go on outside, now." Lorraine knew he should not have done that, so she quickly pushed me out of the store. Like a volcano, I was about to erupt. Lava bubbled in my veins, making my scalp hot enough to straighten my hair! Payback time could not come soon enough.*

*The next time we went to the fountain, I looked at comic books while Lorraine placed her order. First, she asked for a vanilla shake; after the man scooped the ice cream, she sweetly said, "Sir, please excuse me, may I have chocolate instead?" When he turned to put one flavor back and scoop another, I took some of our favorite comic books, ran outside, and waited in the car for Lorraine. After sharing her shake, we went back inside for me to labor over my choice of flavors while she took copies of* True Confessions. *Now, this was not Lorraine's idea, and I regret stealing; but without thinking of the consequences, I felt the need to stand up for what was right, even though it meant doing something wrong.*

*Thank God we weren't caught and that we left Swan Lake before committing another payback. Like when we took fruit from Mr. Flautt's orchard, if Mother had discovered we were on the verge of becoming common thieves, she would have said, "I'll beat the black off you before I let you drag this family's name through the mud." And, she would have whipped us 'til the cows came home. (Except for the cow who came to our house, cows will wander aimlessly until their next milking, which could be a long time, like the following morning.)*

*Though Chuck Berry had not yet recorded the song, his "Memphis Tennessee" expresses our anxiety as Fred carefully drove up Highway 49, the car being so heavily packed he could not make the telephone poles spin. However, the scrumptious Christmas dinner Alice prepared put us all at ease. Why, the aroma of her unforgettable stuffing seems to be wafting through the house; and my tongue is all a-tingling at the thought of those yummy green beans, tasty sweet potatoes, and best-ever banana pudding.*

# To Make
# Her Proud

*A*wakened by Mother's morning prayer, I pulled the
covers over my head to catch a few more winks. Just
as I dozed off, I heard Alice call, "Louise, wake up, baby, so I
can fix your hair. Don't you want to look pretty on your first
day at school?"

Slower than a fractured snail, I rolled out of bed, made
myself presentable, and went into the kitchen for breakfast. By
the time I took my last bite of biscuits and scrambled eggs,
Alice had placed the hot comb on the burner, laid the curlers
aside, and begun to drape a towel over my shoulders. She
brought the ends of the towel to my chest and fastened them
with a clothespin; then she parted my hair to style it in bangs
and a ponytail. After rubbing the hot comb on a piece of cloth
to make sure it was not too hot, Alice gently straightened the
edges of my hair. While she was pressing those at the nape of
my neck, the curlers were heating on the stove.

Every time Alice picked up the hot comb, I flinched, and
she had to remind me to be still so the comb would not touch
my scalp. After she finished the edges, Alice curled the bangs
and the ponytail. Done at last and smiling as she removed the
towel, Alice sent me on my way.

I felt all gussied up in my navy dress with the white collar, white socks, and black and white saddle oxfords. As I was putting on my coat and rushing toward the door, Mother yelled, "Wait a minute! Didn't I tell you I was taking you to school?"

How embarrassing! I knew the way to school and thought I could enroll myself, but Mother insisted on doing so. In our threadbare coats, we shivered all the way to Riverview Elementary School—I was relieved when heat embraced us at the entrance.

Like its exterior, Riverview's interior ran circles around our modest brick school in Swan Lake. The white walls sparkled, the immaculate floors gleamed, and the spacious office glowed, reflecting the elegance of the fashionably and neatly attired principal, Florence Crittenden.

Mrs. Crittenden personified compassion, which made Mother so comfortable she forgot Fred's caution to keep our business to ourselves. After the proper introductions, she talked about how we had moved from Swan Lake with only the clothes on our backs! Then she repeated everything the doctor said about my weak heart. She even told Mrs. Crittenden, "Louise has a sharp tongue, and she's a grade behind, but she's bright and I want her to get a good education." Afflicted with foolish pride, I dropped my head in shame.

Mrs. Crittenden assured Mother she need not worry about my heart, clothes, or education because I would have a good teacher. With an understanding smile, she then complimented me on my pretty dress and added, "One of the new teachers might have clothes your size. If it's okay with you, I'll ask her to bring them."

Mother gave me the "mind your manners" look, and I said, "Yes, ma'am, thank you."

Having completed my enrollment, Mother thanked Mrs. Crittenden for her time, patted my head, and reminded me to be a good girl. After we said our goodbyes, Mrs. Crittenden took me down the hall and tapped on the door of a classroom on my right. A man came out and my eyes twinkled when I heard her say, "Louise, this is your teacher, Mr. White."

My first male teacher! I nodded with a broad closed-mouth smile. Then the two of them turned to the side and began speaking in hushed tones. I knew my place, so I stepped away and looked down the corridor.

After they had finished their conversation, Mrs. Crittenden wished me a good day. Mr. White showed me into the classroom and introduced me to the class. I said "Good morning" and walked toward a desk directly in front of me.

"Oh no, Louise," Mr. White exclaimed, "don't sit there." He pointed toward the right side of the room. "Sit over here."

His desk was at the front of the room, to the right near the door. The desks on the left side of the room were in front of a wall of windows, and they faced the door; the ones on the right faced the teacher's desk. I took an aisle seat in the third row.

Watching him conduct the class, I began to feel slighted. My tongue was sharper than my brain, but I was not exactly slow. From how he interacted with the students, I knew they were seated by ability: the faster learners on the left side of the room and the slower ones on the right.

I wondered if he seated me on the right because I was a year older than most six graders, or because he simply assumed I was slow. Maybe he did so because I was from Mississippi, which had a reputation as the most backward state in the country—but not in my eyes.

Near the end of the day, Mr. White selected a story for the class to read. After everyone on the left side of the room had read, he looked at me. "Louise, would you like to read?"

Wearing the mask, I answered, "Yes, sir."

As was customary in Swan Lake, I stood and read, but not exactly like I did for Miss Rachel or Mrs. Carr who knew and respected my ability. I read as if I were auditioning for the role of a lifetime.

As I was taking my seat, Mr. White smiled and pointed to the left side of the room.

"Oh, oh, Louise, come sit over here." Then he told the class, "Now you see, boys and girls, that is how you all should read."

Whatever his first impression of me may have been, my reading won his respect, and I vowed to keep it by studying hard and always coming to school prepared.

A few days later, Mr. White told me to stop at Mrs. Crittenden's office after he dismissed the class. True to her word, Mrs. Crittenden introduced me to Miss Brown, a petite teacher who had brought a bag of clothes for me. Some of the garments were too big, but with nips and tucks, a few blouses, skirts, and sweaters fit quite well. I particularly loved a brown, tan, and black plaid skirt with a matching brown sweater set. But after tripping on the long skirt on the playground, I put it away until the ninth grade. Though I waited a long time to wear it, the skirt served me well in high school and in college.

By spring, Lorraine and I had adjusted to our new schools. Mother was working two to three days a week, but W C was still unemployed. He began applying for jobs shortly after his seventeenth birthday, but his baby face brought more rejections than did lack of experience. Unable to do anything about his youthful appearance, he inflated his age.

Thinking W C was nineteen, one of Fred's neighbors referred him to Rick's, a restaurant in downtown Memphis. Offered the position of busboy at a salary of $17.50 per week plus tips, W C gladly accepted. Despite—or perhaps, I should say, because of—his handsome baby face, he soon caught the eye of an older white waitress. Smitten, she arranged for him to clear the tables assigned to her. Next thing he knew, she was sharing her tips with him—and her affection too.

To bypass Jim Crow laws, she had W C come to her house as a handyman. After she started calling him at home, Fred lit into W C: "Why did you give that white woman this number? Don't you realize when those people see you going in or coming out of her house all times of day and night, they know you ain't no handyman? You better stop this foolishness before you get yourself killed!"

Now, W C didn't give our phone number to the lady; she probably got it from the restaurant. What's more, he was strong from dragging up to 300 pounds of cotton a day and surely could have taken care of himself, but he stopped going to her house because he knew Fred was right. A few weeks before Fred's warning, a fourteen-year-old Negro from Chicago named Emmitt Till had been kidnapped and murdered in Money, Mississippi, twenty miles from Swan Lake. Emmitt was killed because a young white woman told her husband the boy had made a pass at her when he bought bubble gum at the store the couple owned—a lie she admitted to when she became an old lady. Had W C been caught with his waitress friend, he could have been arrested, charged with rape, and incarcerated, which not only would have possibly ruined his life, it would have prolonged our stay with Fred and Alice even longer.

✺

WITH THE END of our first year in Memphis approaching—
and despite their combined earnings— Mother and W C had
not been able to save enough for our own apartment. So W C
sought a second job at the Hotel Tennessee across the street
from Rick's. After striking up a conversation with a friendly
face, he was hired on the spot for the night shift.

In addition to his position as a dishwasher, he did anything
that needed to be done, not only in the kitchen, but anywhere
in and around the hotel. Impressed by his initiative, the chef
mentored W C. Soon, he was preparing meals that landed him
a promotion to short-order cook. With his increase in salary,
we were able to end our extended stay with Fred and Alice.

To the best of my memory, we lived with them from early
December in 1954 through late spring of 1956. During that
time, I think Mother became suspicious of my fantasies about
Nat King Cole. I had kept our "engagement" a secret after
Lorraine's comments about his age, but seeing how I swooned
every time Nat sang to me from the radio, Mother said it was
time I repent and be saved.

In August, 1955, I attended Bethlehem Baptist Church's
annual revival, a week of services for people—particularly
twelve-year-old children—who had not accepted Christ to
confess, be baptized, and thereby become Christians. At the
front of the sanctuary, a pew called the mourners' bench was
reserved for individuals like me who wanted to repent—and I
certainly did. How I prayed, asking God to forgive me for all
my evil thoughts, bad words, and wrongdoings! Kneeling in
prayer one evening, I felt my body separate: one part seemed
to disintegrate on the bench while the other floated in the air
like an angel. I cannot fully describe the sensation, but the image of rising and floating in the air with the wings of an angel
has never left me. At that moment of separation, tears flowed

because I knew God had forgiven me. So did Mother. I heard her say, "Thank you, Jesus! She's saved."

The first Sunday in September, I was baptized in the pool beside the choir loft.


SEVERAL MONTHS LATER, Mother was walking home from the bus stop when a for-rent sign in front of a lovely white house on Ingle Avenue caught her eye. Stopping to inquire and finding the rent affordable, she paid the first month's rent for a two-room reddish-brown shack in the rear. Unfortunately, the house was not far removed from a cabin on slave row, and we moved into it before the mice moved out. I nearly had a fit!

Always mindful of my weak heart, Mother soon found a gray three-room shotgun house with a half bath—a room with a sink and a commode. Located on the corner of Silver Age and Pennsylvania, the house sat on a hill, with a mulberry tree looming in the front yard and a row of elms dotting the back. We rented the two front rooms and shared the half bath with the couple who lived in the one behind it. Because we had to enter the "bathroom" from an exterior door, if the door was locked, we were glad not to have waited until the last minute, especially in inclement weather.

Shortly after settling into our new home, I completed the seventh grade at Florida Street School, totally unaware that I had been taught by the wife of Benjamin Hooks (1925–2010), one of the attorneys who worked with Thurgood Marshall (1908–1993) on *Brown* v. *the Board of Education* (1954). To tell the truth, I didn't know about the case either.

What was the case? Well, let's take two steps back.

In 1890, Louisiana passed a law ordering "separate but equal" railway cars for white and Negro passengers. To challenge the statute, Homer A. Plessy (1862–1925), a Creole-Negro who was fair enough to "pass," took a seat in the "whites only" railway car. His "racial identity" was discovered; and because Plessy refused to move to the "colored" car, he was arrested, tried, and found guilty. Subsequently, he sued the presiding judge, John Howard Ferguson (1838–1915). *Homer A. Plessy* v. *John Howard Ferguson* (commonly known as *Plessy* v. *Ferguson*) went all the way to the Supreme Court, with the court ruling in Ferguson's favor.[1] However, the ruling was reversed in *Brown* v. *Board of Education of Topeka* (1954).[2]

*Brown* is one of five cases the Supreme Court consolidated under the name *Oliver Brown et al.* v. *the Board of Education Topeka*. Although each case differed in some way, plaintiffs in Kansas, Delaware, South Carolina, Virginia, and the District of Columbia petitioned the court with the same civil rights allegation: state-sponsored racially segregated schools violated the Constitution. *Brown* was put first to show that segregation was not exclusive to the South.

In Kansas, cities such as Topeka with a population over 15,000 could legally maintain separate grade schools for black and white students. Horrified by the conditions of the "all-black" elementary school her colored maid's daughter attended in Merriam, Kansas (Johnson County), Jewish activist Esther Brown (1917–1970) appealed to the school board in 1948.[3] The board's response—installing new light bulbs, but no indoor toilets—sent her straight to the local chapter of the NAACP. She then raised money to sue the Merriam Kansas School Board in *Webb* v. *School District No. 90 Johnson County*. In 1949, the Kansas Supreme Court ruled in her favor, declaring that separating students by race was unlawful.

Encouraged by the ruling, Brown partnered with the NAACP to help Oliver Brown and twelve other parents file a class-action suit against the Board of Education of Topeka. The "whites only" school seven blocks from Oliver Brown's home refused to admit his third-grade daughter Linda, forcing her to walk six blocks to take a bus to a "blacks only" school about a mile away.

The NAACP assigned Thurgood Marshall to represent the group. Marshall—who became the first African American Supreme Court justice in 1967—was the lead attorney in the team of lawyers who prepared the brief for the consolidated cases. Although Marshall presented data showing separate schools made black children feel inferior, he based his argument for declaring segregation illegal on the "equal protection clause" in the Fourteenth Amendment to the Constitution. *Brown* v. *Board of Education* is among the twenty-nine of thirty-two cases Marshall argued before the Supreme Court and won.[4]

Citing a belief in the inferiority of Negroes as the only reason to support segregation, Chief Justice Earl Warren (1891–1974) persuaded the two dissenting justices to join the court in a unanimous decision that declared segregation in public schools unconstitutional. However, it took over fifteen years, another Supreme Court ruling that ordered desegregation "with all deliberate speed," busing black students to previously whites-only schools, and even murder before all states in the country desegregated most of their schools.

Memphis began to integrate its schools in October 1961, when thirteen Negroes enrolled in the first grade at four previously whites-only elementary schools. Five years later, all twelve grades and faculties were desegregated, but only a handful of colored students attended some of the previously "white" schools.

Negroes in Mississippi feared challenging the status quo, save for World War II veteran and civil-rights activist Medger

Evers (1925–1963). Following the *Brown* decision, Evers tested the ruling by applying to the segregated University of Mississippi Law School. After his admission was denied, Evers became the first field secretary for the NAACP in Mississippi. Despite threats on his life, he organized voter registration drives, boycotts of white-owned companies that discriminated, and investigations of crimes against blacks.

One evening, when he returned home without the usual FBI and police escorts, a racist white carried out the threat: On June 12, 1963, Evers was killed by a white supremacist whose first two trials resulted in hung juries. In 1994, a third trial produced a conviction and a sentence of life imprisonment. About seven years later, he died at the age of eighty. His name was deliberately omitted so as not to tarnish this book.

Some historians consider the Brown case as the formal beginning of the Civil Rights Movement; however, the years 1955–1964 are used because protests for African Americans' equal protection, as stated in the Constitution, escalated after Rosa Parks (1913–2005) refused to give her seat to a white passenger on December 1, 1955. The movement is too vast for this discussion, so I offer a brief sketch.

With "We Shall Overcome" as their anthem and non-violent civil disobedience via boycotts, sit-ins, and voter registration drives as ammunition, black and white civil-rights workers defeated armies of whites who carried the most lethal weapons of all: ignorance and hatred. It has been said that segregation may have lingered indefinitely without the internationally televised images of America at its ugliest—racist mobs jeering at a black child as she is escorted to school by federal marshals in 1960; a governor declaring in 1963, "segregation now, segregation tomorrow, segregation forever"; and policemen billy clubbing marchers, spraying them with tear gas, and drenching them with fire hoses. The nine-year battle for equal opportunity ended with President Lyndon Johnson (1908–1973) signing into law on July 2 the Civil Rights Act of 1964, which:

- banned discrimination based on race, color, religion, gender, or national origin
- mandated equal access to public places and employment
- ordered enforcement of desegregation of schools and of the right to vote

After Negroes organized the Montgomery Bus Boycott, rumors of one in Memphis reached our neighborhood. Had there been a boycott, Mother would have depended on church members who formed carpools to go to and from work. She always stood up for what was right, regardless of the costs. Remember how she forced the Flautts to pay J C?

Growing up on a farm, with the exception of the incident at the soda fountain, I had not experienced discrimination like my classmates in Memphis. Negroes were the majority in Swan Lake; except for the Flautts, the only contact I had with white people was on occasional trips to the movies in Webb. The first and only public school in Swan Lake was the brick school that opened for us in 1950. When I asked why a bus took Jack Flautt's daughter to another school and not us, I was told not to ask such a question—a response typical of the ways parents and other adults protected us from the irrationality of racism.

I didn't know Negroes were admitted to the museum on specific days because we went to town only on Saturdays—to see a movie or to shop. And hamlet that it was, Webb had neither a zoo nor a museum. In addition, neither our church school nor the public school provided field trips. The train was the only public transportation Mother used, and I did not see riding in a car with only colored people as discriminatory because most of the people in Swan Lake were colored. In Memphis, I simply walked every place Mother allowed me to go: church and school.

And how she emphasized school, often saying, "I want someone in this family to get some learning, make something of themselves, and make me proud." Of course, she loved and was proud of each of us; this was merely her way of encouraging Lorraine and me to take advantage of the opportunities her adult offspring did not have. We attended class the entire school year, and our schools in Memphis were better equipped than the one-room church school our older siblings attended, but for only about four months each year.

Lorraine did her best at Booker T. Washington High School; and I did well at Florida Street School, especially under the tutelage of Mrs. Hooks and my eighth grade homeroom teacher Mrs. Westbrook, a well-groomed, gracious, and proper lady who made English easy to learn.

Petite and always stylish, Mrs. Hooks seated us in alphabetical order by last name, not by ability. And she never said a word about my being a grade behind. Matter of fact, after I memorized and recited an assignment, she called me smart. Of course, memorizing was easy for me, but I would not call understanding only 13 percent of what I read smart. However, reading was my favorite subject because I believed if I could think of a question, there was a book with the answer, especially about how cleanliness prevents the spread of germs and disease.

As you will recall, I repeated the fourth grade because of my obsession with neatness. Well, in the eighth grade, that obsession and my respect for Mrs. Westbrook saved me from an after-school brawl. No way would I behave in a way that reflected poorly on my family or on Mrs. Westbrook.

Before school closed in 1957, a classmate told me Jessie Mae, known to be "bad," was going to beat me up after school. Allegedly, Jessie Mae had said she was tired of my big mouth and of me, always raising my hand as if I thought I knew more than everyone. She mistook my impatience for arrogance.

Anyhow, Jessie Mae dressed well and wore a different— and equally pretty—dress every day. Like most of my classmates, she wasn't nearly as small as I. So yes, she had the advantage of size, but like she said, I had a big mouth.

Sure enough, the next day, Jessie Mae and a group of students were waiting for me about two blocks down the street from school. When I didn't step off the sidewalk to walk around them, they moved as if they were going to let me pass. Instead, they formed a circle around Jessie Mae and me. Trying to ignore her, I said, "Excuse me," but someone started egging Jessie Mae on, and she got right up in my face. Now, that was too close! As you'll recall, I need my space. But I knew if I moved, one of her cronies was sure to push me toward her. Thus, if the principal heard about the fight, Jessie Mae could say I hit her first. So, I stood my ground.

"Jessie Mae," I said, "you always look so nice. But if you touch me, your pretty dress is going to get real dirty because you and I are going to roll all over this filthy sidewalk and onto the grass. I don't want that to happen, and I'm sure you don't either. Besides, your mother will be upset if you come home with this expensive dress all dirtied, ripped, and torn."

Although it was not my intention, Jessie Mae apparently saw the mention of her mother as playing the dozens. Stunned, and no match for my big mouth, instead of throwing a punch she stepped around me and started walking up the street toward her home. With a silent sigh of relief, I continued down the road to mine.

BY SPRING OF 1957, thirteen of us lived in the house on Silver Age. First, Linda asked Mother if she and her six children could come and live with us until she found an apartment, then Cousin Rebecca made the same request for herself and her teenage son Oliver. Mother said yes to both of them, and when I objected, she reminded me how Fred and Alice had shared their home with us. Then she made it clear we had an obligation to do the same for any relative who needed our help.

Eventually, we all moved to separate apartments, with Mother making 165 Vaal Avenue home for her, W C, and me. This move was quite an improvement, but I found myself becoming increasingly distressed over Mother's endless struggle to provide for us. Making matters worse, I began to question my ability to get a college education that would enable me to take care of Mother, and still fulfill my dream of marrying Nat King Cole and traveling the world with him.

Such was my frame of mind when Cousin Rose, a lifelong pupil of piano, introduced me to classical music, beginning with Tchaikovsky's *Piano Concerto No.1 in B-flat Minor*, followed by Debussy's *Claire de Lune*, and Beethoven's *Moonlight Sonata*. Cousin Rose was a refuge for me during my teens, always giving the best advice: Recognize when someone does not know any better and do not expect more from anyone than he or she can do. If at a loss for words, which was rare, Cousin Rose quoted passages from Ralph Waldo Emerson's *Self-Reliance* and Edgar Guest's *Myself*, her favorite poem. Why, she even had her children memorize the poem, which in her late eighties, she could still recite flawlessly. Knowing how much I studied, she was disappointed when my senior class voted me "most sophisticated" instead of "most studious."

The voting was fine with me because I knew the truth. I may have been more sophisticated than a rutabaga, but I was not naturally studious like my friend Annie Doris who won the title. Now, I like acquiring knowledge, but with an erratic IQ, I had to study hard to make grades good enough to earn academic scholarships, the only means of going to college and living the life of my dreams. Four years as a high school "senior" prepared me for those scholarships, and for college. Allow me to explain.

In September 1957, George Washington Carver Junior High School opened with grades seven through nine, adding a grade each year to make Carver a junior-senior high school: the ninth grade became the tenth, which became the eleventh then the twelfth. A ninth-grader when school opened, I was considered a "senior" then and each of the following three years.

Most of the high school teachers were recent college graduates, so those in their first year of teaching were only a few years older than we students, which made it easier for them to relate to us. But none of them related to me better than the home economics teacher, Mrs. Evie Horton. She overlooked my sharp tongue, but not my attention to detail. I would remove and reinsert a zipper or sleeve, or undo and resew a seam until I got it right.

At the beginning of my sophomore year, Mrs. Horton asked my permission to enter me in a sewing contest at the Memphis-Shelby County Fair. Having never been to a fair or won a contest, I was apprehensive and fearful of disappointing Mrs. Horton. However, after she assured me the fair was nothing to be afraid of and that I could win up to ten dollars for putting a zipper in a skirt, I gladly gave my permission.

When I arrived at the fair and saw more people, animals, and activities than I had ever seen, my stomach was all aflutter. But Mrs. Horton's gentle smile calmed my nerves and steadied my hands. Blocking out everything around me, I sat at the sewing machine, pinned, and basted the zipper. Checking each stitch, I was almost finished when I noticed what appeared to be a slight pucker.

Panic stricken, I glanced at Mrs. Horton. The look in her eyes said, "You can do it!" So I did. What a thrill it was to accept the first place ribbon and ten dollars! The money paid for my home economics' supplies, another pair of penny loafers, and a few other items, but it was not enough to cover lunch money. Fortunately, I had found a part-time job during the summer.

With eleven years of experience babysitting gratis, I felt qualified to apply for a salaried position in July 1958. I had no references, but I had something better: my mother's reputation. Mother told me to ask for Mrs. Matthews at the employment office and to introduce myself as "Lula Blocker's daughter." I obeyed her and found Mrs. Matthews to be as proficient for me as she had been for Mother. In no time at all, she found a job order from a Mrs. Frager, whom she called right in front of me.

"Years ago," Mrs. Matthews told Mrs. Frager, "this girl's mother came to me with the best letter of recommendation, and on every job I sent her, she did well. Like her mother, Louise is well groomed and respectful. She's a tenth-grader with an excellent report card and experience babysitting."

She paused as Mrs. Frager spoke and my weak heart sped up, but I smiled to calm it down.

"Yes," Mrs. Matthews replied, "when can you interview her?"

Continuing to smile, I waited.

"Thursday? Wonderful!"

My heart leapt after Mrs. Matthews hung up the phone and gave me the directions.

This time, I disobeyed Mother. Instead of going to the back door like she told me, when I went for the interview, I walked up the driveway to the front door and rang the doorbell. With a beautiful smile and a warm hello, Mrs. Frager (Natalie) opened the door, invited me in, and showed me to a seat in the living room. She and Mr. Frager (Jerry) needed a sitter for their Saturday night dinner date. After a slew of questions, she hired me to babysit from noon on Saturday until noon on Sunday.

From then on, I worked overnight every Saturday—and occasionally, from Friday evening through Sunday night. Sometimes I wrapped bags of coins Jerry brought home from his coin-operated laundry. By the end of my first two months with the Fragers, I had saved enough for lunch money, school supplies, a pair of white penny loafers, material, and supplies for home economics.

When school started in 1958 and each year thereafter, Mother did not have to buy my school clothes or give me money for lunch—which most of the time in previous years, she simply did not have. Again, Mrs. Horton entered me in the county fair's sewing contest. After putting a so-so sleeve in a dress, I walked away with five dollars and a ribbon for second place. First place the next year would have been mine, but school assignments and work prevented me from competing. After rushing home from school, I had to hit the books and do chores.

Speaking of rushing home, I was doing precisely that when Jawbone, known to be the leader of a gang, tried to strike up a conversation with me. (If I remember correctly, he was called Jawbone because his punch was hard enough to break the jaw.) Repulsed by his reputation, I ignored him and started walking faster. Jawbone did not like that! He stepped in front of me, raised his hand, and slapped me so hard the print of his palm was still on my face when I got home.

Mother took one look at me and asked, "What happened to your face? Did somebody hit you?"

"Yes, ma'am. Jawbone slapped me because I wouldn't talk to him."

"Where does he live?" she asked.

"I don't know," I answered honestly. "But please don't do anything because Jawbone carries a knife, and he may cut me the next time."

Mother fumed. "There won't be no next time because Jawbone is going to jail."

With that, she went next door to use the neighbor's telephone to call the police. When the officers took our complaint and asked for the boy's name, I said, "They call him Jawbone."

The policemen looked at each other and smiled. One of them said, "We know who he is. Now, don't you worry, we'll get him."

A few weeks later, we met Jawbone in court. After I testified, Mother asked the judge if she could have a word. The judge said "Yes," and I thought, *Someone should call an ambulance because Jawbone is about to get cut real bad.*

When Mother got up, Jawbone dropped his head. "Oh no, you don't," she said. "If you so bad, why can't you look at me? Raise your head and look me in the eye! I want you to see me and mark my every word. You better not never ever dare to put your hands on my child again! You hear me? You have some nerve! You ought to be ashamed of yourself, walking around with a knife trying to scare people. Well, I ain't scared of you, and I'll pray for you." Mother glanced at the judge, then back at the gangster. "But I want the judge to lock you up and keep you in jail 'til you learn your lesson. You have no right to harm anybody."

Realizing her time was up, Mother sat down. Jawbone was sentenced and taken to jail, and I never saw him again.

After Mother's performance in court, I was more committed than ever to make her proud, which meant I had to study even harder. Consequently, I read while I rode the bus to and from work on weekends, and I studied when the boys took a nap and after I put them to bed for the night. Sometimes, I studied until just before the Fragers came home from their dinner date. Once or twice, I was still studying when they came into the house. Instead of telling me the lack of sleep could render me unfit to care for their children, they understood.

The Fragers were also quite generous.

Periodically, they added a gratuity to my salary. When I told Natalie I was not going to my senior prom because I could not afford to buy a formal, she went to her closet, pulled out a gorgeous gown, and gave it to me. And when Jerry learned that instead of the traditional valedictorian's speech, students from the speech class would speak at Carver's commencement, he was visibly shaken. His face flushed, he said, "Louise, you studied so hard and made the grades that earned you the title and the right to give the speech. I'm going to the school to have a talk with the principal."

"Please don't do that," I said. "I really appreciate your kindness, but it will only make matters worse."

I knew venom would have been spewed if a white man had gone to Carver and spoken on my behalf. Impatient, sharp tongued, and lacking time to socialize, I was considered a snob. My classmates had no idea that working on the weekends, hitting the books after school, and doing chores at home left no time for me to hang out with them, go to movies and parties, or participate in any other teenage activities. At school, I associated with a select group of friends, primarily Annie Doris, June Katherine, and Zadie Marie who became my best forever friends, and now my divinest Ya Ya sisters.

As for the valedictorian's speech, receiving scholarships for the distinction was more important to me than making a speech. Little did I know the title would also give me my first fifteen minutes of fame. The *Memphis Press-Scimitar* and *The Commercial Appeal* ran articles about me as valedictorian of Carver's first graduation class, winner of a one-year $200 Sears & Roebuck Scholarship, and first recipient of a $400 Marie P. Lowenstein Scholarship, renewable for three years contingent on my maintaining a B average. Topping it off, I was accepted by the college of my choice before I even applied.

A few weeks after my interview for the Lowenstein Scholarship, Dr. Albert Dent, the president of Dillard University, was attending a seminar in Memphis. One of the gentlemen who interviewed me arranged for him to meet me.

A tall imposing man, Dr. Dent began with Dillard's history and proceeded with its focus on academics, the renowned nursing program, and the student selection process. The interrogation followed:

*Why did I choose Dillard?*
*What could I offer?*
*What course of study would I pursue?*
*How would I pay tuition?*
*Would I live on campus?*
And so on.

Satisfied with my answers, he ended the meeting with a handshake and a welcome to Dillard University, indicating the paperwork could come later.

With enough scholarships for one year at Dillard—tuition, room, and board were $1,000 dollars—I had to find a summer job to earn money for train fare, books, and miscellaneous items. Of course, I went back to Mrs. Matthews. Reviewing her job requests, she found one that matched my experience: a helper at Mrs. Tudd's Child Care Center. Early the next morning, I left home for the interview.

When I rang the front doorbell, Mrs. Tudd directed me to come in through a side door. From there, we went into the kitchen. She offered me a seat, explained the center's operations, and described my duties as a helper, beginning that very day. With only two months to work before leaving for college, I was happy to earn an extra day's pay.

Showing me to a tiny room in the basement, Mrs. Tudd said, "You can change into your uniform here, use the toilet, and freshen up at the sink."

*No way!* I thought. *I'll wear my uniform to work and avoid this dank area as much as possible.*

Later in the afternoon, Mrs. Tudd told me that her daughter, who had stopped by, worked at the center periodically because she was having financial and marital problems.

On my third Thursday at the center, the thought of going into the basement sent my colon into spasms so painful that I had to go home shortly after lunch. The next day, Mrs. Tudd met me at the door.

"You stole five dollars," she said, pointing to a wall table in the foyer. "The money was on this table when you arrived yesterday, but not there after you left." Before I could refute her accusation, she added, "The theft has been reported to the police, and an officer is on his way to arrest you."

What a shock! While I stood in the foyer proclaiming my innocence, a car pulled into the driveway. In no time at all, an officer had pounced up the steps, opened the door, and was ordering me to come with him.

Horrified, I followed him outside, and when he told me to get into the patrol car, I protested. "Sir, I will not get into that car to be taken to jail for something I didn't do."

Stunned, the officer snapped, "Don't tell me what you won't do. You'll do what I say. Now go on, get in the car."

Overpowered, I followed his order and sat in the back. He got into the car and turned to me. "You want to tell me why you took the money?"

Fighting to control my rage and to preserve my future, I answered, "I have scholarships for college, which I plan to leave for in a few weeks. I would not risk that by stealing. Besides, for the last three years I have babysat overnight every weekend for a family who owns a laundromat. That man brings home bags of coins for me to count and put into wrappers. Now, why, when I have access to hundreds of dollars, would I steal five?"

Obviously an astute detective, the officer muttered, "So you didn't take the money?"

At that point, I put on the mask and with the utmost respect replied, "No, sir, I did not."

Rubbing his chin, he paused for a moment, then opening the car door said, "Wait here," and went into the house.

After a few minutes—during which I saw my future evaporate, with me sitting in a jail cell instead of in a college classroom—he returned with the accuser.

Looking like she had been put in her place, Mrs. Tudd said, "Well, this officer has convinced me you didn't take the money, so come on inside, and we'll just forget about it."

"No, ma'am," I said, "I'll never forget this, and I won't work here any longer. I cannot work for anyone who doesn't trust me."

She smirked. "Don't be foolish and throw away another chance to make money you need for college."

In that moment, I wanted to grab her and shake some

sense into her head. Instead, I removed the mask, looked straight into her eyes, and had my say.

"Money isn't as important as respect. Saying you're giving me a second chance when I have done nothing wrong is not only disrespectful, it is deceitful as well."

Mrs. Tudd's eyes widened. Having been told off by a ninety-eight-pound colored girl, she stood aghast as I turned and went down the driveway to the bus stop, walking like Mother did on her way to Sumner. I imagine the cracks in the sidewalk quivered as I stepped over them.

Of course, I went back to Mrs. Matthews. And knowing Mother and me, she disregarded whatever tale Mrs. Tudd may have concocted. She found another position, which I kept until mid-August. Adding the salary to my earnings from the Fragers gave me enough money to purchase incidentals and a set of luggage that Jerry's friend sold to me at a discount.

On my last weekend at the Fragers before I left for college, Natalie gave me a gorgeous emerald green semi-formal dress. "You might need it," she said. And I did—as a contestant for the Miss United Negro College Fund. No, I did not win, but I felt beautiful in the dress.

To my surprise, Natalie and the three boys were waiting to see me off to college when I arrived at Central Station to take the train to New Orleans. There was no doubt that their hugs and love made the nine-hour ride less taxing.

ENTERING DILLARD'S CAMPUS, I was greeted by bright white buildings: Rosenwald and Stern Halls at the front, the elegant library and male dormitories on the left side of the campus, the student union and dining hall centered at the end, and the female dorms on the right. A row of trees lined two sidewalks, one on each side of a green median known as the Avenue of Oaks. A flagpole with a flag flying stood at the rotary in the middle of the campus. Rows of pink, white, and lavender azaleas surrounded each building, and perfectly manicured lawns adorned the entire campus. I thought it was the most beautiful place I had ever seen. (I soon learned only the gardeners were allowed to walk on the grass.)

Inspired by the campus, I registered feeling confident in my ability to renew the Lowenstein Scholarship with a B average. To cover the additional fees for three years, I would apply for a National Defense Student Loan and an academic scholarship. For personal expenses, I would work on campus. With my registration complete, and with applications for the loan and scholarship in hand, I was ready to tackle my classes.

During the first lecture of freshman English, however, I found my Lowenstein Scholarship in jeopardy. The white professor, Dr. Barnes—who was a British citizen—announced, "No one in this class will receive a B. The best students will make a C, many will barely pass with a D, and some will fail."

Feeling worse than a declawed cat, I left Dr. Barnes's class and went to the library. When my eyes met those of the cute assistant librarian, I took that as a cue, introduced myself, and inquired about a job. After consulting with the head librarian, he hired me. Hooray! The only thing left was to prove Dr. Barnes wrong.

Recalling my first day at Riverview Elementary School, I vowed to always come to class prepared, turn in every paper before its due date—with no dangling participles, no lack of parallelism, no mixed metaphors, every modifier properly placed, and every infinitive together. In addition, I would include humor in my essays and be the last to answer questions or make comments in class. I figured I could count on my erratic IQ to differentiate my inquiries, which, by coming at the end of the session might have a lingering, and hopefully, positive effect on Dr. Barnes.

At the end of the second semester, my request for an annual National Defense Student Loan had been honored, and having earned a B in English both semesters, the Lowenstein Scholarship was out of jeopardy. My application for an academic scholarship, however, had not even been acknowledged, leaving me short of the amount I needed for each of the next three years. Disappointed and doubtful of ever finishing college, I went home for the summer and returned to my job at the Fragers. Lo and behold, in mid-July, I received a letter from Dillard: the university had granted me a three-year academic scholarship!

Upon hearing my good news, the Fragers thought it should be shared with the entire community. Jerry presented my quest for a college education as a timely human interest piece to the editor of our local newspaper, *The Commercial Appeal*. The editor sent Angus McEachran (1939–2018) to interview me at the Fragers' home.

I received my second, and probably last, fifteen minutes of fame when *The Commercial Appeal* published McEachran's summary of the interview with my age inflated by two years, a picture of me standing beside an ironing board, the iron in one hand and a book in the other. Subscribers from all over the Southeast sent me cards and letters of congratulations. Some even sent checks, which, added to the National Defense Student Loan and the academic scholarships covered most of the fees for my last three years of college.

Certain the earnings from my part-time job in the library would pay for incidentals, I was eager to begin my sophomore year. A few days after returning to Dillard, however, just as I awoke from a dream in which my sister Lorraine had died, the pay telephone in the hall rang. I thought, *That's Mother calling to tell me Lorraine is dead.*

There was a knock on the door, and someone yelled, "Louise, long distance."

I rushed to the phone so Mother would not have to pay for more minutes than necessary. Ever mindful of my weak heart, she began, "Now don't you get too nervous and upset over what I'm about to tell you. But . . . I think you need to come home. Your sister Ethel has been shot and is no longer with us."

I couldn't believe it. In my dream, it had been Lorraine, but with as much calm as I could muster, I said, "Mom, I already know from a dream. I'm so sorry. Please don't worry about me. I'm all right, and I'll tell you more about the dream when I get home. I'll be there as soon as I can."

Wondering if the shooting occurred while I was dreaming, I hung up the phone. Later, I learned that Lorraine had heard gunshots, and as she approached Ethel's room, the assailant aimed his pistol at her. The gun either misfired or had no more bullets, at which point the man fled. But he was later arrested and brought to justice: life imprisonment for first degree murder.

Using the ticket set aside to go home for the Christmas holidays, I left New Orleans the day after the dean approved my absence for a week. Understandably, I boarded the train not only grieving but also conflicted. How would missing a week of classes affect my grades? How could I stretch my budget to buy another round-trip ticket? Would I have to remain on campus during the holidays?

But, as faith would have it, I should not have worried at all. Like she usually did, Mother had been praying: when I got home, more letters and checks, forwarded by *The Commercial*

*Appeal,* were waiting for me. There was also a package from Mrs. J.M. Ray, a childless, elderly white woman who lived in Sulligent, Alabama. The large box was filled with clothes, a knitted turquoise and white throw, and assorted snacks. For three years, Mrs. Ray mailed encouraging letters, care packages, and clothes to me. We kept in touch until the late 1960s.

Mother often said, "Where there's a will, there's a way." By God's grace, I had the will and found a way to complete my college education. On May 31, 1965, I marched down the Avenue of Oaks to receive my Bachelor of Arts Degree cum laude. With a Peace Corps assignment waiting for me in Columbia, South America, I was ready to "Change the World."

But I would have to do so without Nat King Cole (March 17, 1919–February 15, 1965).

## ♫ Accompaniments ♫

*With the faith expressed in "Only Believe," as sung by Mahalia Jackson, I boarded the train for New Orleans. In my purse, I carried a thumbnail Bible that contained one of my favorite passages, Psalm 121:*

*I will lift up my eyes to the hills—*
*From whence comes my help?*
*My help comes from the Lord,*
*Who made heaven and earth.*
*He will not allow your foot to be moved;*
*He who keeps you will not slumber.*
*Behold, He who keeps Israel*
*Shall neither slumber nor sleep.*

*The Lord is your keeper;*
*The Lord is your shade at your right hand.*
*The sun shall not strike you by day,*
*Nor the moon by night.*

*The Lord shall preserve you from evil;*
*He shall preserve your soul.*
*The Lord shall preserve your going out and your coming in*
*From this time forth, and even forevermore.*

*During my four years at Dillard, I lifted up my eyes three times a week at mandatory chapel and on Sundays during Vespers. Like at home, Dillard did not allow its students to wear "everyday clothes" to Vespers or to Sunday dinner.*

*To ensure freshmen were in good health, Dillard arranged for residents from Meharry Medical School to give each student a complete physical examination. Fearing my weak heart would raise a red flag, I was a bundle of nerves while waiting for the doctor. Finally, with a folder in his hand, he entered the room, exclaiming, "Louise Blocker, I know you! My sister-in-law talks about you all the time. What a pleasure to meet you!" The doctor was Benjamin Hooks's brother. His pleasure at meeting me was met by my embarrassment of being partially disrobed. Fortunately, he found me physically fit, but had he checked the mind . . .*

*A poor country girl working my way through college, I did not participate in protests during the Civil Rights Movement: I thought joining the NAACP was the best way to support the cause. However, when the representative took exception to my disapproval of welfare for unwed mothers of more than one child, I withdrew my application.*

*To become a well-rounded "Dillard woman," I was obliged to complement the spiritual life of chapel and Vespers with a university-approved social life of activities and events held on campus: basketball and football games, theater, an occasional movie, and mandatory formal and semi-formal dances. In the second semester of my sophomore year, I attended the dances with a freshman whom a friend introduced to me as one of my admirers.*

*A flattering, smooth-talking basketball player, the admirer was a superb dancer. Although one foot, two inches taller than I, he stood erect and glided me around the floor so well I never missed a step! By my senior year, we had fallen in love with love and claimed "My Girl" by the Temptations as our song. His voice was that of an anchorman, but his intellect made him the best stand-in for Nat King Cole.*

# Postlude ↙

Visiting over 81,000 years of history, though invigorating, was at times infuriating enough to compromise my objectivity. Consequently, instead of presenting merely the facts, I at times editorialized more than was necessary, which merely illustrates that, like vice and virtue, good intentions do not discriminate. All three are found among all Homo sapiens—regardless of so-called race, ethnicity, or culture.

African slave dealers—also called drivers—partnered with Arabic and European slave traders; whites were conductors on the Underground Railroad; and they taught at Negro schools, colleges, and universities. Self-taught, my ancestors and my siblings contributed to the nation's economy as servants, skilled laborers, craftsmen, entrepreneurs, educators, and property owners. Female and male descendants of both slaveholders and slaves supported the 1955–1964 Civil Rights Movement. Indeed, God has blessed America and I am grateful.

In like manner, I appreciate a dinosaur-days childhood that allowed me to roam safely through fields and pastures, walk miles on dirt and gravel roads, recite poems and pray in school, and watch tadpoles and minnows play in creeks. But, like the dinosaur, the climate of my youth is extinct. Hurry the day when corporal punishment disappears too!

Writing this book transported me back not only to the

period, place, and people of dinosaur days but also to the language. Adages, idioms, and phrases of the time seemed to spontaneously appear on a page, and I left them there. However, I refrained from using dialect, not only because I do not know how to, but also because jargon is inappropriate for today's readers. What's more, writing in dialect may reinforce both the use of non-standard English and the stereotypical image of a people whose diction was the result of being denied the formal education their vision opened doors for me to receive.

I attended segregated public schools and matriculated at what was then known as a Negro college. Now it is one of the Historically Black Colleges and Universities (HBCU). Most of my professors at Dillard were white, and although they showed no particular bias, their instruction was from a white perspective: not only were they white, so were the authors who wrote the textbooks they used.

Of the seventy-nine authors on the "Freshman Reading List," four were African American males: W.E.B. DuBois, Alexandre Dumas, Langston Hughes, and Richard Wright, with only one book by each. Seeing the drama department's production of Lorraine Hansberry's *A Raisin in the Sun,* I realized the extent of my miseducation.

Immediately after graduation, I began to reeducate myself by collecting and reading books written by and/or about African Americans. Later, I added authors from other ethnic groups, particularly Asian, Hispanic, Italian, and Jewish. The collection was an invaluable reference for this book. The Internet was a handy fingertip resource, but I cross-checked my findings on at least three credible websites, giving preference to educational institutions, reputable periodicals, the Public Broadcasting System, civil rights organizations, and governmental agencies.

I am pleased to have finished this book in less than thirteen years—a number that has been a recurring one in my life since the day I was born:

I became the thirteenth member of my immediate family.

The seven letters in my surname and the six in my given name equal thirteen.

By choosing to repeat the fourth grade, I spent thirteen years in grade school instead of the usual twelve.

We moved to Memphis with only $13.05.

At the age of thirteen, I became a Judeo-Christian.

I began my career with Stuart Pharmaceuticals on September 13, 1982.

Stuart became AstraZeneca after changing its name and merging with Astra in 1999, a company established in 1913.

Mother died on May 13, 1991.

August 13th is Left-Handers Day.

I imagine Lamin is "Dancing on the Ceiling." As for me, I have to take two pairs of thirteen-minute naps before attempting to answer any more questions.

## ♫ Accompaniments ♫

Stevie Wonder's "Superstition" expresses the common perception of the number thirteen.

"I Remember, I Believe," by Lizz Wright, answers the unasked questions about fun during slavery.

"I Hope You Dance," as sung by Oleta Adams, is my wish for youths, and for grandmothers too. It is better to take a chance and do something that may be right than do nothing and risk becoming a passive perpetrator or innocent victim of something that is definitely wrong.

# ENDNOTES

## WHO WE ARE

[1] Gould, Stephen Jay. *Discover Magazine*. New York: Time Inc., November 1, 1994.

[2] Bhopal, Raj, Bruce Usher, and John Usher. London: BMJ 2007: 335:1308. December 20, 2007.

[3] Smedley, Audrey. "The Rise of Science: Early Attempts to Classify Human Population" in *Race in North America – Origin and Evolution of a Worldview*. Colorado: Westview Press. 2007, p. 169.

[4] Ibid. 172.

[5] Jackson, John G. "Ethiopia and the Evolution of Civilization" in *Introduction to African Civilizations*. New York: Citadel Press, 2001, pp. 90–91.

## THE EVOLUTION OF AMERICAN SLAVERY

[1] Segal, Ronald. "People" in *The Black Diaspora*. New York: The Noonday Press. Farrar, Strauss and Giroux, 1966, pp. 3–14.

[2] Bennett, Lerone, Jr. "The African Past" and "Before the Mayflower" in *Before the Mayflower: A History of the Negro in America 1619–1964*. Rev. ed. New York: Penguin Books, 1969, pp. 3, 5–29.

[3] Ibid, p. 34.

[4] Cooke, Alistair. "A Passage to America" in *Alistair Cooke's America*. New York: Alfred A. Knofp, 1973, pp. 15–16.

[5] Ibid.

[6] Brodie, James Michael. "Slave Inventors" in *Created Equal: The Lives and Ideas of Black American Innovators*. New York: William Morrow and Company, Inc., 1993, p. 25.

## WHENCE AND HOW THEY CAME

[1] Garraty, John A. and Peter Gay. "Sub-Saharan Africa" in *The Columbia History of the World.* New York: Harper & Row, Publishers, 1972, p. 301.

[2] Jackson, John G. "Ethiopia and the Origin of Civilization" in *Introduction of African Civilizations.* New York: Citadel Press, 2001, p. 91.

[3] Hochschild, Adam. "Many Golden Dreams" in *Bury the Chains: Prophets and Rebels in the Fight to Free an Empire's Slaves.* Boston and New York: Houghton Mifflin Company, 2005, p. 17.

[4] Bennett, Lerone, Jr. "Before the Mayflower" in *Before the Mayflower: A History of the Negro in America 1619–1964.* New York: Penguin Books, p. 40.

[5] Ibid, p. 41.

[6] Harris, Middleton, Morris Levitt, Roger Furman, and Ernest Smith. *The Black Book.* New York: Random House, 1974, p. 15.

[7] Hochschild, Adam. "A Tale of Two Ships" in *Bury the Chains: Prophets and Rebels in the Fight to Free an Empire's Slaves.* Boston and New York: Houghton Mifflin Company, 2005, pp. 79–82.

[8] Bender, Andrew. "Memphis Tells Our Story." *Los Angeles Times.* February 7, 2016.

[9] Bennett, Lerone, Jr. "Before the Mayflower" in *Before the Mayflower: A History of the Negro in America 1619–1964.* New York: Penguin Books, p. 30.

[10] Hughes, Langston, Milton Meltzer, and C. Eric Lincoln. "How We Came to America" in *A Pictorial History of Black Americans.* Fifth Rev. ed. New York: Crown Publishers, Inc., p. 10. And Washington Post.com. History, "The Slave Who Found a New World." Sunday, December 4, 2008. And http://washingtonpost.com/wp_dyn/content/article/2008/12/11AR2008121102957.html

[11] Woodson, Carter G. "How We Drifted from the Truth" in *The Mis-Education of the Negro.* Virginia: Khalifah's Booksellers & Associates, 2005, p. 21.

## MOMENTS OF JOY

[1] Harris, Middleton, Morris Levitt, Roger Furman, and Ernest Smith. *The Black Book*. New York: Random House, Inc. 1974, p. 30.

[2] National Public Radio. "The Banjo's Roots Reconsidered" on "All Things Considered," August 23, 2011.

[3] Painter, Nell Irvin. "Isabella's New York City" and "Akron 1851." In *Sojourner Truth: A Life, A Symbol*. New York and London: W.W. Norton & Company, Inc. 1997, pp. 33–34, 58, 75.

[4] Kantor, Susan. "Songs and Poetry" in *African-American Read Aloud Stories*. New York: Black Dog & Leventhal Publishers, Inc. 1998, pp. 300, 301, 413.

## ADAPTING AND ESCAPING

[1] Newman, Richard and Marcia Sawyer, PhD. "From Resistance to Reconstruction 1776–1877" in *Everybody Say Freedom: Everything You Need to Know About African-American History*. New York: The Penguin Group, 1996, p. 81.

[2] PBS.org. "Levi Coffin's Underground Railroad Station" in *Africans in America*.

[3] Katz, William Loren. "Slavery in the West" in *The Black West*. Washington: Open Hand Publishing Inc., 1987, p. 97.

[4] PBS.org. "Henry 'Box' Brown" in *Underground Railroad: The William Still Story*. 90th Parallel Productions Ltd. In association with Rogers Broadcasting Limited and WNED-TV Buffalo/Toronto.

[5] Ibid, pp. 63–64. And Holmes, Marian Smith. "The Great Escape from Slavery of Ellen and William Craft." Smithsonian.com. June 16, 2010.

[6] Harris, Middleton, Morris Levitt, Roger Furman, and Ernest Smith. *The Black Book*. New York: Random House, Inc., 1974, p. 10.

7 Blassingame, James. "American Freedmen's Inquiry Commission Interviews, 1863" in *Slave Testimony: Two Centuries of Letters, Speeches, Interviews, and Autobiographies.* Louisiana: Louisiana State University Press, 1977, pp. 682–86.

8 Ibid, p. 686.

9 Katz, William Loren. "The Early Settlers" in *The Black West.* Washington: Open Hand Publishing, 1987, p. 73.

10 Painter, Nell Irvin. "Akron, 1851." In *Sojourner Truth: A Life, A Symbol.* New York: W. W. Norton & Company, 1997, p. 125.

## FLIGHTS AND FIGHTS FOR FREEDOM

1 Garraty, John A. and Peter Gay. "The Jews in Medieval Europe" in *The Columbia History of the World.* New York: Harper & Row, 1972, p. 423.

2 Hofstadter, Richard, William Miller, and Daniel Aaron. "A Violent Decade" in *The United States: The History of a Republic.* New Jersey: Prentice-Hall, Inc., 1963, p. 31.

3 "British Troops Deploy" in *Founding Fathers: America's Great Leaders and the Fight for Freedom.* Washington: National Geographic Partners, 2016, p. 17.

4 Bennett, Lerone J. "The Negro in the American Revolution" in *Before the Mayflower: A History of the Negro in America 1619–1964.* New York: Penguin Books, 1970, p. 58.

5 Ibid, p. 59.

6 Kantor, Susan. "Black Heroes of the American Revolution" in *One Hundred and One African-American Read-Aloud Stories.* New York: Black Dog & Leventhal Publishers, 1998, p. 307.

7 Ibid, p. 308.

8 Burns, James McGregor and Jack Walter Peltason. "Immigrants, Aliens, and Citizens in *Government by the People: The Dynamics of*

*American, National, State, and Local Government.* New Jersey: 1964, pp. 207–10.

9 Brandon, Williams. "The Dispossessed" in *Indians.* New York: Houghton Mifflin Company, 1987, pp. 236–37.

10 Hofstadter, Richard, William Miller, and Daniel Aaron. "A Violent Decade" in *The United States: The History of a Republic.* New Jersey: Prentice-Hall, Inc., 1963, p. 220.

11 Pauls, Elizabeth Prine, "Trail of Tears" in *United States History.* Online: Encyclopedia Britannica. August 6, 2018.

12 Hofstadter, Richard, William Miller, and Daniel Aaron. "A Violent Decade" in *The United States: The History of a Republic.* New Jersey: Prentice-Hall, Inc., 1963, p. 261.

13 Ibid.

14 Woodson, Carter G. *The Mis-Education of the Negro.* Virginia: Khalifah's Booksellers & Associates, 2008, p. 99.

15 Johnson, Charles and Patricia Smith. "The People Speak" in *Africans in America: America's Journey Through Slavery.* New York: Harcourt Brace & Company, 1998, pp. 285.

16 McLaurin, Melton A. *Celia, a Slave: A True Story.* New York: Perennial, an Imprint of HarperCollins Publishers, 2002.

17 "Reclaiming Nat Turner" in *History.* Washington: National Geographic Partners, 2017, p. 79-81.

18 Ibid. p. 79.

19 cop.senate.gov/art and history. December 11, 2018.

20 Hofstadter, Richard, William Miller, and Daniel Aaron. "A Violent Decade" in *The United States: The History of a Republic.* New Jersey: Prentice-Hall, Inc., 1963, p. 344.

21 Ibid. 295–96.

22 www.abrahamlincoleonline.org/lincoln/speeches/greeley.htm (accessed August 6, 2018).

23 Ibid.

24 National Archives. The Emancipation Proclamation. Page 1. Record Group 11. General Records of the United States.

25 https://hampton.gov/1912/history (accessed August 6, 2018).

26 Leveen, Lois. "The Opinion Page" in *The New York Times*. June 21, 2012.

27 Hofstadter, Richard, William Miller, and Daniel Aaron. "Reconstruction and the South" in *The United States: The History of a Republic*. New Jersey: Prentice-Hall, Inc., 1961, pp. 388–89.

28 Ibid.

29 Bennett, Lerone J. "Black Power in Dixie" in *Before the Mayflower: A History of the Negro in America 1619–1964*. New York: Penguin Books, 1969, p. 198.

30 Ibid, pp. 184–86.

31 Hughes, Langston, Milton Meltzer, and C. Eric Lincoln. "The Roots of Jim Crow" in *A Pictorial History of Black-Americans*. New York: Crown Publishers, Inc., 1973, p. 39.

## STONY THE ROAD

1 Washington, Booker T. "Early Days at Tuskegee" in *Up from Slavery, the Autobiography of Booker T. Washington*. New York: Carol Publishing Group, 1989, p. 108.

2 Newman, Richard and Marcia Sawyer, PhD. "From the Nadir to the New Negro, 1878–1919" in *Everybody Say Freedom, Everything You Need to Know About African-American History*. New York: The Penguin Group, 1996, p. 154.

[3] Ascoli, Peter Max. "Youth and First Business Ventures, 1862–1895" in *Julius Rosenwald: The Man Who Build Sears, Roebuck and Advanced the Cause of Black Education in the American South.* Bloomington, Indiana: University Press, 2006.

[4] Ibid. "Blacks, Politics, and Philanthropy, 1908–1912. And http://www.sjlmag.com/2012/06/conference-to-celebrate-rosenwalds.html (accessed July 2017).

[5] Newman, Richard and Marcia Sawyer, PhD. "From the Nadir to the New Negro, 1878–1919" in *Everybody Say Freedom, Everything You Need to Know About African-American History.* New York: The Penguin Group, 1996, pp. 155–56. And http://www.sjlmag.com/2012/06/conference-to-celebrate-rosenwalds.html (accessed July 2016).

[6] Brodie, James Michael. *Created Equal: The Lives and Ideas of Black American Innovators.* New York: William Morrow and Company, Inc., 1993, p. 61.

[7] www.brooklynrail.net/Granville_woods.html (accessed January 2018).

[8] Biography.com. *Elijah McCoy Biography.* The Biography.com website. A&E Television Networks. 2018.

[9] Newman, Richard and Marcia Sawyer, PhD. "From the Nadir to the New Negro, 1878–1919" in *Everybody Say Freedom, Everything You Need to Know About African-American History.* New York: The Penguin Group, 1996, p. 157.

[10] Hughes, Langston, Milton Meltzer, and C. Eric Lincoln. "The Roots of Jim Crow" in *A Pictorial History of Black-Americans.* New York: Crown Publishers, Inc., 1973, p. 252.

[11] http//www.naacp.org/history-of-lynching/(accessed 1/01/2019).

[12] Ibid.

[13] Newman, Richard and Marcia Sawyer, PhD. "From the Nadir to the New Negro 1878–1919" in *Everybody Say Freedom: Everything You Need to Know About African-American History.* New York: Penguin Books, 1996, pp. 217.

## PATHS TO MISSISSIPPI

[1] Hofstadter, Richard, William Miller, and Daniel Aaron. "Reconstruction and the South" in *The United States: The History of a Republic*. New Jersey: Prentice-Hall, Inc., 1963, pp. 391.

## SHE KEPT US TOGETHER

[1] American Chemical Society International Historic Chemical Landmarks. Discovery and Development of Penicillin. http://www.acs.org./content/acs/en/education/whatischemistry/landmarks/flemingpenicillin.html (accessed August 16, 2016).

[2] Mississippi History Now. "German Prisoners of War in Mississippi, 1943–1946." An online publication of the Mississippi Historical Society (accessed April 16, 2015). http://.k12.ms.us/articles/233/german-prisoners-of-war-in-mississippi-1943-1946.

[3] Edgerton, Robert B. "Made Perfect Fools of Themselves" in *Hidden Heroism Black Soldiers in America's Wars*. New York: Barnes & Noble, Inc., by arrangement with Westview Press, 2001, p. 142.

[4] Ibid, p. 145, and Hughes, Langston, Milton Meltzer, and C. Eric Lincoln. "The Roots of Jim Crow" in *A Pictorial History of Black-Americans*. New York: Crown Publishers, Inc., 1973, p. 294.

[5] National Archives. www.//.archives.gov/education/lessons/japanese-relocation "Japanese Relocation During World War II" (accessed March 15, 2017).

[6] Ibid.

## EIGHT DOLLARS AND FIVE CENTS

[1] Katz, William Loren. "The Black Infantry and Calvary" in *The Black West*. Washington: Open Hand Publishing Inc., 1987, p. 210.

[2] Ibid, p. 151.

## TO MAKE HER PROUD

1 http://www.pbs.org/wnet/supremecourt/antebellum/ landmark_plessy.html (accessed April 10, 2015).

2 National Archives. Brown v. Board of Education of Topeka: A Landmark Case Unresolved Fifty Years Later. Spring 2004, Vol. 36, No. 1 by Jean Van Delinder.

3 https://www.nps.gov/ "The Segregation of Topeka's Public School System, 1879–1951 (accessed April 10, 2015). And NPS and USA Today Network. McAtee Cerbin, Carolyn. USA Today. "Kansas Housewife Stood Up to Segregation Injustice." February 3, 2017.

4 Lacayo, Richard. "The Good Fight" in *Time Special Edition: Thurgood Marshall, the Visionary.* New York: Time Inc., Specials, 2017, p. 6.

# BIBLIOGRAPHY

Ascoli, Peter Max. *Julius Rosenwald: The Man Who Built Sears, Roebuck and Advanced the Cause of Black Education in the American South.* Bloomington: Indiana University Press, 2006.

Bennett, Lerone, Jr. *Before the Mayflower: A History of the Negro in America 1619–1964.* Rev. ed. New York: Penguin Books, 1970.

———. *The Shaping of Black America: The Struggles and Triumphs of African Americans, 1619 to the 1990s.* New York: Penguin Books, 1993.

Bible. Ex. 20: 1–17, Mark 3: 24–25.

Blacker, Irwin R., *Prescott's Histories: The Rise and Decline of the Spanish Empire.* New York: Dorset Press, 1963.

Blassingame, John W. *Slave Testimony: Two Centuries of Letters, Speeches, Interviews, and Autobiographies.* Baton Rouge: Louisiana State University Press, 2012.

Brandon, William. *Indians.* Boston: Houghton Mifflin Company, 1987.

Brodie, James Michael. *Created Equal: The Lives and Ideas of Black American Innovators.* New York: William Morrow and Company, Inc., 1993.

Broyard, Bliss. *One Drop: Father's Hidden Life – A Story of Race and Family Secrets.* New York: Back Bay Books/Little, Brown and Company, 2007.

Burns, James MacGregor and Jack Walter Peltason. *Government by the People.* Englewood Cliffs, Prentice Hall, 1964.

Byrd, Rudolph P., *The Essential Writings of James Weldon Johnson.* New York: The Modern Library, 2008.

Chase-Riboud, Barbara. *Echo of Lions.* New York: William Morrow and Company, Inc., 1989.

Cooke, Alistair. *Alistair Cooke's America.* New York: Alfred A. Knopf, 1973.

Cooke, Jean, Ann Kramer, and Theodore Rowland-Entwistle. *History's Timeline.* New York: Crescent Books, 1981.

Davis, Edwin Adams and William Ransom Hogan. *The Barber of Natchez.* Baton Rouge: Louisiana State University Press, 1973.

Diop, Cheikh Anta. *Precolonial Black Africa.* Chicago: Lawrence Hill Books, 1987.

Douglass, Frederick. *Narrative of the Life of Frederick Douglass, an American Slave.* New York: Doubleday, 1973.

Du Bois, W. E. B. *The Souls of Black Folk.* New York: Bantam Books, 1989.

———. *The Gift of Black Folk.* Garden City Park: Square One Publishers, 2009.

Edgerton, Robert B. *Hidden Heroism: Black Soldiers in America's Wars.* New York: Barnes & Noble, Inc., by arrangement with Westview Press, 2001.

Garraty, John A. and Peter Gay. *The Columbia History of the World.* New York: Harper & Row, 1972.

Gombrich, E.H. *A Little History of the World.* New Haven and London: Yale University Press, 2008.

Harris, Middleton, Morris Levitt, Roger Furman, and Ernest Smith. *The Black Book.* New York: Random House, Inc., 1974.

Hochschild, Adam. *Bury the Chains: Prophets and Rebels in the Fight to Free an Empire's Slaves.* Boston and New York: Houghton Mifflin Company, 2005.

Hofstadter, Richard, William Miller, and Daniel Aaron. *The United States: The History of a Republic.* Englewood Cliffs: Prentice Hall, Inc., 1957.

Huffman, Alan. *Mississippi in Africa.* New York: Gotham Books, a division of Penguin Group (USA) Inc., 2004.

Hughes, Langston, Milton Meltzer, and C. Eric Lincoln. *A Pictorial History of Black-Americans.* New York: Crown Publishers, Inc., 1983.

Johnson, Charles, Patricia Smith, and the WGBH Series Research Team. *Africans in America: America's Journey Through Slavery.* New York: Harcourt Brace & Company, 1998.

Kantor, Susan. *One Hundred and One African-American Read-Aloud Stories.* New York: Black Dog & Leventhal Publishers, Inc., 1998.

Kaplan, Carla. *Zora Neale Hurston: A Life in Letters.* New York: Doubleday, 2002.

Kontos, Peter G., Linda L. Rogers, Cecille P. Kontos, et al., *Patterns of Civilization: Africa.* New York: Cambridge Book Company, 1975.

MacAustin, Hilary and Kathleen Thompson. *The Face of Our Past: Images of Black Women from Colonial America to the Present.* Bloomington: Indiana University Press, 2009.

Manis, Jerome G. and Samuel I. Clark. *Man and Society: An Introduction to Social Science.* New York: The Macmillan Company, 1960.

McLaurin, Melton A. *Celia, a Slave: A True Story.* New York. Perennials. 2002.

Mississippi History Now. "German Prisoners of War in Mississippi, 1943–1964," an online publication of Mississippi Historical Society.

Mitchell, James, Editor in Chief, and Jess Stein, Editorial Director. *The Random House Encyclopedia.* New York: Random House, Inc., 1977.

Morrison, Toni. *Beloved.* New York: Alfred A. Knopf, 1987.

Newman, Richard and Marcia Sawyer, PhD. *Everybody Say Freedom: Everything You Need to Know About African American History.* New York: Penguin Books, USA Inc., 1996.

Painter, Nell Irvin. *Sojourner Truth: A Life, A Symbol.* New York and London: W.W. Norton & Company, Inc., 1997.

Paragon. *American History.* Bath BA 1HE UK: Parragon Books Ltd., 2011.

———. *World History.* Bath BA 1HE UK: Parragon Books Ltd., 2011.

Pickard, Kate E.R. *The Kidnapped & The Ransomed: The Narrative of Peter & Vina Still After Forty Years of Slavery.* Lincoln and London: University of Nebraska Press, 1995.

Robeson, Paul. *Here I Stand*. Boston: Beacon Press, 1988.

Segal, Ronald. *The Black Diaspora*. New York: The Noonday Press, Farrar, Straus and Giroux, 1996.

Shannon, David A. *Twentieth Century America: The United States Since the 1890s*. Chicago: Rand McNally & Company, 1963.

Spalding, Henry D. *Encyclopedia of Black Folklore and Humor*. New York: Jonathan David Publishers, Inc., 1993.

Styron, William. *The Confessions of Nat Turner*. New York: Random House, 1967.

Tucker, Phillip Thomas. *Cathy Williams: From Slave to Buffalo Soldier*. Mechanicsburg. Stackpole Books. 2009.

Woodson, Carter G. *The Mis-Education of the Negro*. Drewryville: Khalifah's Booksellers & Associates, 2008.

# ACKNOWLEDGMENTS

"And a little child shall lead them."
*Isaiah 11:6*

Having talked about writing a book for decades, I thank God for the gift of the pen and for Lamin, whose curiosity and sensitivity made me close my mouth and make these pages talk.

For their encouragement, expertise, and patience, I give a bouquet of gratitude to Doris Spearman, Ilene Roper, Lenore Dollries, Mary Blanton, Ernestine Washington, Stacey Aaronson, Stephanie Dougherty, Eván Weekes, Linda Gordon, and Barbara Glass.

To my dear brother W C, I thank you for your confidence, encouragement, and wisdom. I applaud you for the exceptional man you came to be.

And to the reader, I appreciate your time and hope you found it well spent. If you have questions, I encourage you to explore the Internet while you listen to the music—that is, if you are not dancing.

# ABOUT THE AUTHOR

𝓛𝓸𝓾𝓲𝓼𝓮 𝓑𝓵𝓸𝓬𝓴𝓮𝓻 spent her formative years on the farm where she was born in Swan Lake, Mississippi, and her teens in Memphis, Tennessee. Her education began in a church that served as a one-room schoolhouse. She went on to receive her Bachelor of Arts degree from Dillard University in New Orleans, Louisiana.

Her career as a language arts and social studies teacher in Chattanooga, Tennessee, ended when she began a westward migration—first to Lawrence, Kansas, then a step back to Kansas City, Missouri, before continuing on to Southern California. In 1991, she became the founder, editor, and publisher of *CONTACT*, the Blocker family's newsletter. Her "Blocker Family Prayer" and "1994 Blocker Family Reunion Prayer" are published in *Book of Prayers* by Holman United Methodist Church in Los Angeles, California.

The divorced mother of one son, grandmother of one grandson, and aunt to four generations of nieces and nephews—553 in 2018— Louise enjoys music, literature, films, theater, and Sudoku.

CPSIA information can be obtained
at www.ICGtesting.com
Printed in the USA
FSHW011359061119
63760FS